Speed Reading

My special thanks are due to Mr. Robert Millard-Smith for many detailed suggestions, to Joy Buttery, my Personal Assistant, whose devotion and willingness to work far beyond the normal call of duty enabled me to meet the deadline, and to my friend Heinz Norden whose personal guidance has proved invaluable.

Speed Reading

Tony Buzan

David & Charles
Newton Abbot London North Pomfret (Vt)

British Library Cataloguing in Publication Data
Buzan, Tony
  Speed reading.
  1. Rapid reading
  I. Title
  428.4'3   LB1050.54
  ISBN 0-7153-7366-8

Previously published in 1971 by
Sphere Books Limited

© Tony Buzan 1971
  Revised and updated 1977
  Third impression 1981
  Fourth impression 1982

Printed in Great Britain
by A. Wheaton and Co. Ltd Exeter
for David & Charles (Publishers) Limited
Brunel House   Newton Abbot   Devon

Published in the United States of America
by David & Charles Inc
North Pomfret   Vermont 05053   USA

EDITOR'S FOREWORD

It is a privilege to commend this book to the great army of people, young and old, who are eager to master more knowledge of our exasperating and endearing world—the heritage of the past, scientific and political developments of the day, current and classical literature. It marks the emergence of a brilliant young man, Tony Buzan, whose career I have, in a modest way, been trying to foster for several years and who is rapidly making a name for himself.

Tony Buzan here reduces to a simple and easily followed learning system what I and my contemporaries had to acquire painfully and empirically—if we acquired it at all. Let me assure you that using this system you will swiftly equal if not exceed what I have had to do for many years: read at least three newspapers a day; some 25 scientific journals, half a dozen general weeklies and two or three books each week; and about a dozen general magazines each month—as well as many letters, reports, clippings, references, handbooks, catalogues, etc.

I could wish that I had years ago enjoyed the benefit of the system Tony Buzan here sets forth so lucidly. It would have saved me much lost effort, many wasted moves; and I am not a bit ashamed to admit that even today I continue to learn from him how to do still better. You are likely to have the advantage of starting out on the right foot at a much earlier stage. I plead with you to seize the opportunity! It will require effort, even with Tony Buzan's clearly explained step-by-step system; but if you persevere, you will find that this book is like the opening of a door into a world thick with the golden sunshine of knowledge.

Heinz Norden
Fellow of the Institute of Linguistics
Editorial Director, The Portland Group.
Erstwhile Information Editor, The Book of Knowledge.

TABLE OF CONTENTS

7

PREFACE

As most readers will be aware the field of speed reading itself has contributed to the recent print explosion. Almost as soon as we were swamped with books to read, we were swamped with books on how to read them! Unfortunately many of these books were written by people with no real qualification in the fields of Education, Psychology, and Reading in particular. This book will therefore take issue with much of what has been published up to the present time, and will present new theories and explanations on such major areas as vocalising while reading, study methods, back-skipping and regression, finger pointing, skimming and scanning, and comprehension. A number of other out-of-date concepts will be explained in the light of the most recent research.

Reading—A Necessity

In recent years the volume of magazines and books pouring off the international presses has reached almost unmanageable proportions, and a number of steps must be taken to meet this rising flood.

This fantastic growth of reading material is obvious enough, but what is overlooked is that there are *no known limits* to the capacity of the human mind. There are today more 'well-informed' people than ever, i.e. people who know a great deal about a great many things. In fact, the 'generalist' (as opposed to the 'specialist') has made a startling come-back. Scientists and leaders in all fields have come to realise that they cannot function effectively in the modern world without knowing a great deal not only about their own special field of interest, but about a broad range of related subjects—in fact just about everything. Yesterday's specialist, defined as 'a man (or woman) who knows more and more about less and less,' has given way to an eager host of young people who want to 'know more and more about more and more' and are realising precisely this ambition.

How do they do it? It is not just a matter of mobilising the huge reserve capacity of the human mind. *Technique* is all-important—how to absorb, master, integrate and retain knowledge most expeditiously and efficiently. A key element in acquiring these skills is to *increase reading efficiency.* You do not have to be a genius to appreciate that if you could read twice as efficiently as you now do, you could go through twice as much reading material in the same time.

I want to emphasise strongly that it is not very difficult to learn to read faster, if you are determined—but as one who has spent years teaching and practising the art of efficient-reading it is my contention that most of the books on the subject are not worth the paper they are printed on.

It goes without saying that 'speed'-reading is utterly pointless if you *do not understand or cannot remember what you read.* All speed-reading methods recognise that and use so-called 'Comprehension tests' to check that you actually have understood and retained what you have read, to make certain that your comprehension keeps pace with your growing speed. *But this is not enough.* Quite apart from important improvements in the technique of learning how to read fast which are set forth in this book, what I wish to emphasise in my system is that *understanding and remembering factual material* is not nearly as important as knowing how to *relate new material to what you already know.* This is the all-important 'integrative factor', or if you will, *learning how to learn.* You cannot 'look up' *perspective, inter-relation, or how to make a consistent, coherent meaningful pattern of everything you know and learn.* Facts alone are dead things. It is how you put them together, how you use them, that counts in getting ahead in the modern science-oriented world.

This book will not only teach you how to read faster but how to make something of everything you have ever read or will ever read.

Self Tests and Exercises

In certain chapters are special exercises designed to increase your facility in visual perception, mental awareness and critical ability. There is also a programmed series of articles and selected readings designed to give you a continuing indication of your progress through the book.

These readings are not simply interesting items that have been selected at random, but are a series dealing with the theories and history of the major areas of human knowledge. By the time you have finished the book you will therefore not only have increased your reading speed, maintained your comprehension, and improved your critical and appreciative abilities, but will also have been given a very general education in subjects ranging from Art and Music through Psychology to Astronomy and the current thought on the nature of the Universe.

How to Read

Having mentioned the print explosion and the similar explosion in better reading books, I have now added to that total myself. To atone for this sin I offer an approach to SPEED READING which will aid the reader to complete it as efficiently as possible. The suggestions that I shall make now will, of course, be explained in greater detail later especially in the chapter on the Buzan Study Technique, but even now they will aid you enormously as you progress.

Having read the preface, go through the table of contents thoroughly, mapping out the territory you wish to cover. Then roughly plan the time period you will devote to each section of the book, finishing with a general outline in your mind's eye of both the content and the programme of study for that content.

After this, browse (but fairly quickly!) through the book, familiarising yourself with the different sections, and adding to the mental picture already developed by the table of contents. Before each chapter-reading a quick refresher-browse will help to re-familiarise you with the material that is about to be covered, and will make the whole reading task far easier and more enjoyable. Try to complete one chapter every 3 days, practising your newly acquired techniques in between chapters.

CHAPTER ONE

INTRODUCTION

In this chapter I ask you to do exactly the *opposite* of what I shall be asking you to do in every other chapter! I ask you *not* to speed, because this reading is to give an indication of what your normal reading speed is. If you go faster than you are accustomed to you will not be able to judge accurately the progress you make throughout the book, and will not really know your present reading level. Comprehension will also be tested. It should be the kind of comprehension you get when normally reading this type of material.

Don't worry about getting low scores in either speed *or* comprehension. Remember that this book has been written for people who want to improve their reading skills and that low initial scores are not only common, they're expected.

Right then, no dashing along for higher than usual speeds, no plodding for super comprehension scores, and no worrying about your result. Have your watch by your side, do your reading privately (someone timing you or watching you inevitably disturbs comprehension and tends to make some people read more hurriedly than usual, others more slowly) and start a *normal* reading on the following passage *now*.

SELF TEST 1
THE METHODS OF SCIENCE
Observation and Experiment

The methods used by working scientists have evolved from a separation of methods used in ordinary life, particularly in the manual trades. First you have a look at the job and then you try something and see if it will work. In more learned language, we begin with observations and follow with *experiments*. Now everyone, whether he is a scientist or not, observes; but the important things are what to observe and how to observe them. It is in this sense that the scientist differs from the artist. The artist observes in order to transform, through his own experience and feeling, what he sees into some new and *evocative creation*. The scientist observes in order to find things and relations that are as far as possible independent of his own sentiments. This does not mean that he should have no conscious aim. Far from it: as the history of science shows, some objective, often a practical one, is almost an essential requirement for the discovery of new things. What it does mean is that in order to achieve its goal in the inhuman world, deaf to the most emotional appeal, desire must be subordinated to fact and law.

Classification and Measurement

Two techniques have in time grown out of naive observation: *classification and measurement*. Both are, of course, much older than conscious science, but they are now used in quite a special way. Classification has become in itself the first step towards understanding new groups of phenomena. They have to be put in order before anything can be done with them. Measurement is only one further stage of that putting in order. Counting is the ordering of one collection against another; in the last resort against the fingers. Measuring is counting the number of a standard collection that balance or line up with the quantity that is to be weighed or measured. It is measurement that links science with mathematics on the one hand, and with commercial and mechanical practice on the other. It is by measurement that numbers and forms enter science, and it is also by measurement that it is possible to indicate precisely what has to be done to reproduce given conditions and obtain a desired result.

It is here that the active aspect of science comes into the picture—that characterized by the word 'experiment'. After all, as the word indicates, it is only a trial, and early experiments indeed were full scale trials. Once measurement was introduced it was possible not only to reproduce trials accurately, but also to take the somewhat daring step of carrying them out on a small scale. It is that small-scale or model experiment that is the essential feature of modern science. By working on a small scale far more trials can be carried out at the same time and far more cheaply. Moreover, by the use of mathematics, far more valuable results can be obtained from the many small-scale experiments than from one or two elaborate and costly full scale trials. All experiments boil down to two very simple operations: taking apart and putting together again; or in scientific language, analysis and synthesis. Unless you can take a thing or a process to bits you can do nothing with it but observe it as an undivided whole. Unless you can put the pieces together again and make the whole thing work there is no way of knowing whether you have introduced something new or left something out in your analysis.

Apparatus

In order to carry out these operations, scientists have, over the course of centuries, evolved a complete set of material tools of their own—the *apparatus* of science. Now apparatus is not anything mysterious. It is simply the tools of ordinary life turned to very special purposes. The crucible is just a pot, the forceps a pair of tongs. In turn, the apparatus of the scientist often comes back into practical life in the form of useful instruments or implements. It is not very long, for instance, since the modern television set was the cathode-ray tube, a purely scientific piece of apparatus devised to measure the mass of the electron. Scientific apparatus fulfils either of two major functions: as scientific instruments, such as telescopes or microscopes, it can be used to extend and make more precise our sensory perception of the world; as scientific tools, such as micro-manipulators, stills, or incubators, it can be used to extend, in a controlled way, our motor manipulation of the things around us.

Laws, Hypotheses, and Theories

From the results of experiments, or rather from the mixture of operation and observation that constitutes experiments, comes the whole body of scientific knowledge. But that body is not simply a list of such results. If it were, science would soon become as unwieldy and as difficult to understand as the Nature from which it started. Before these results can be of any use, and in many cases before they can even be obtained, it is necessary to tie them together, so to speak, in bundles, to group them and to relate them to each other, and this is the function of the logical part of science. The arguments of science, the use of mathematical symbols and formulae, in earlier stages merely the use of names, lead to the continuous creation of the more or less coherent edifice of scientific *laws, principles, hypotheses, and theories.* And that is not the end; it is here that science is continually beginning, for, arising from such hypotheses and theories, there come the practical *applications* of science. These in turn, if they work, and even more often if they do not, give rise to new observations, new experiments, and new theories. Experiment, interpretation, application, all march on together and between them make up the effective, live, and social body of science.

The Language of Science

In the process of observation, experiment, and logical interpretation, there has grown up the *language* or rather, the languages, of science that have become in the course of time as essential to it as the material apparatus. Like the apparatus, these languages are not intrinsically strange; they derive from common usage and often come back to it again. A cycle was once *kuklos*, a wheel, but it lived many centuries as an abstract term for recurring phenomena before it came back to earth as a bicycle. The enormous convenience of making use of quite ordinary words in the forgotten languages of Greece and Rome was to avoid confusion with common meanings. The Greek scientists were under the great disadvantage of not having a word—in Greek—for it. They had to express themselves in a roundabout way in plain language—to talk about the submaxillary gland as 'the acorn-like lumps under the jaw'. But these practices, though they helped the scientists to discuss more clearly and briefly, had the disadvantage of building up a series of special languages or jargons that effectively, and sometimes deliberately, kept science away from the ordinary man. This barrier, however, is by no means necessary. Scientific language is too useful to unlearn, but it can and will infiltrate into common speech once scientific ideas become as familiar adjuncts of everyday life as scientific gadgets.

The section that you have just read contained 1,250 words. In order to calculate your words per minute, divide the number of minutes taken to read the article into the number of words. When you have done this, enter the w.p.m. score in your progress graph at the back of the book.

Following are fifteen true or false questions. Circle the word next to the answer you think is correct, and when you have completed all fifteen check your answers with the answers on page 157. With a different coloured pen or pencil enter your comprehension score on the same graph as you have entered your reading score.

w.p.m. ....   comprehension ....

TEST 1

1. Scientific methods were largely based on the observation of manual trades.   True   False
2. The scientist observes and uses his own sentiments in order to find relationships.   True   False
3. Observation has become in itself the first step toward understanding new groups of phenomena.   True   False
4. Science and mathematics are linked by order, not by measurement.   True   False
5. Early experiments were done as full-scale trials.   True   False
6. The small-scale experiment is the essential feature of modern science.   True   False
7. All experiments boiled down to three simple operations.   True   False
8. The one basis for all experiments is synthesis.   True   False
9. Scientific apparatus is derived from and is based upon the needs of science.   True   False
10. The body of scientific knowledge is the product of operation and observation.   True   False
11. Scientific laws and theories are claimed to be the end or goal of science.   True   False
12. Scientific hypotheses but not the applications of science, give rise to new observations and experiments.   True   False
13. The language of science derives from common usage.   True   False

14. The word 'kuklos' has been applied to non-recurring phenomena.   True   False
15. Scientific language has kept science away from the ordinary man.   True   False

CHAPTER TWO

EYE MOVEMENTS

One of the most surprising facts about our eyes is that they see properly *only when fixed* on the object at which they are looking. (Actually the seeing eye is never *entirely* still. It makes minute and imperceptible scanning movements known as 'saccadic' movements, probably to avoid an image falling on the same nerve receptors). We tend to think that they see while moving, when in fact movement creates a blur. As a simple check, watch people in trains or any moving vehicle looking at things outside the window. Their eyes will not simply 'absorb' all that passes by—you will notice an enormous number of tiny movements taking place in which their eyes 'fix' on an object, moves to another and 'fix' on that, and so on.

It is the same with reading. Most people, when asked to describe how their eyes move during the reading process, are likely to say that they glide smoothly over each line, pausing briefly at the end before going back to the beginning of the next. It seems to be a continuous and flowing movement, although many people will admit that their eyes go back over certain words.

In fact the reading process is quite different, and the eye, as it does when seeing anything clearly, takes in the printed information only when it is still. You may well ask 'how can we possibly read at all if the eye takes in the words only when it is still?.'

The answer is that the eyes make small and fairly regular 'jumps'. These take the eye from fixation point to fixation point, usually a bit more than a word at a time.

To sum up, the eye does *not* move smoothly over the page at all, but instead moves in small jerks from left to right, pausing momentarily to take in a word or two before moving on and repeating the process. Perhaps this can be most clearly explained by the use of a diagram:

FIXATIONS

WORDS

Fig. 1   Diagram of the eyes' progression while reading

While the eye is moving and pausing, moving and pausing in this way the information is absorbed, as has been explained, *only during the pauses.* These pauses take up most of the time, and as each pause may last from one-fifth to one-and-a-half seconds, it can be seen that an improvement in reading speed is indeed possible by spending less time on each pause.

Before going on with this however, let us diagram the eye movements of a very poor reader:

BACK-SKIPPING OR REGRESSION

WORD

Fig. 2   Diagram of a poor reader's eye movements

This reader makes about twice as many pauses, or *fixations* as they are commonly called, as does the reader diagrammed in Fig. 1. His extra pauses are caused by the fact that he often re-reads words, sometimes skipping back as many as three places to make sure that he has taken in the correct meaning. These habits of back-skipping (returning, almost as a habit, to words that have just been read) and regression (returning consciously to words which the reader feels he has missed or misunderstood) cause the poor reader's excessive number of fixations as shown in Fig. 2. On a simple mathematical basis, i.e. the addition of the time that he takes for each pause, his reading rate must inevitably be slower.

Now, what about the good reader? Let us diagram his eye movements first and then discuss them, while explaining at the same time how the poor reader can go about improving his own efficiency by eliminating certain bad habits and practising more efficient ones:

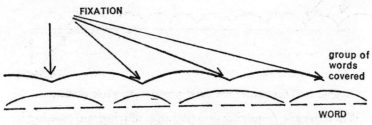

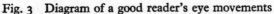

Fig. 3 Diagram of a good reader's eye movements

We immediately see from this diagram that the good reader, while not back-skipping or regressing, has also lengthened his 'jumps'. He no longer takes in a word or a little more at a time but has progressed to being able to take in two or three words at one fixation. If we assume for the moment that each fixation takes the same time, and set that time arbitrarily at $\frac{1}{2}$ second, we can see that his total reading time for eight words is $\frac{1}{2} + \frac{1}{2} + \frac{1}{2} + \frac{1}{2} =$ two seconds, whereas the poor reader, for the same line, takes $\frac{1}{2} + \frac{1}{2} + \frac{1}{2} + \frac{1}{2} + \frac{1}{2} + \frac{1}{2} + \frac{1}{2} + \frac{1}{2} + \frac{1}{2} + \frac{1}{2} + \frac{1}{2} + \frac{1}{2} + \frac{1}{2} + \frac{1}{2} + \frac{1}{2} + \frac{1}{2} =$ eight seconds, or four times as long.

Our first task, therefore, is to work at eliminating these bad habits. Since widening the awareness of the visual span helps eliminate back-skipping and regression, we shall start with that.

The exercises that follow are designed to make you more aware of your own visual span, and will provide motivation for taking in more at a glance as you read. In doing the exercises use a card to cover up the column of numbers. Expose each number *as briefly as possible*, giving yourself no more than a split second to see it, and to see it only once. Almost at the same time as it is uncovered it should be re-covered.

Then write in the space next to the number what you think that number is, and check yourself to see whether you were right or wrong. Continue to the next number, repeating the process until the page has been completed. You will find that the exercise becomes more difficult as you progress, because the number of digits is gradually increased. If you can reach the end of the six-digit numbers without having made any mistakes you will have done extremely well.

25	....	52	....
73	....	78	....
81	....	62	....
90	....	72	....
21	....	52	....
34	....	28	....
65	....	23	....
24	....	30	....
45	....	01	....
12	....	84	....
71	....	42	....
19	....	66	....
49	....	75	....
22	....	05	....
39	....	27	....
95	....	87	....
76	....	83	....
44	....	14	....
20	....	59	....
82	....	48	....
98	....	77	....
57	....	86	....
17	....	02	....
276	....	863	....
832	....	824	....
012	....	952	....
735	....	424	....
225	....	735	....
128	....	489	....
902	....	362	....
270	....	645	....
735	....	725	....

725	....	724	....
875	....	324	....
012	....	634	....
776	....	727	....
227	....	728	....
534	....	752	....
644	....	234	....
189	....	721	....
706	....	853	....
620	....	825	....
525	....	214	....
160	....	711	....
641	....	862	....
394	....	875	....
552	....	112	....
962	....	829	....
629	....	926	....
662	....	929	....
262	....	296	....
723	....	825	....
237	....	258	....
327	....	582	....
727	....	828	....
766	....	765	....
544	....	165	....
112	....	865	....
751	....	755	....
678	....	753	....
552	....	102	....
012	....	214	....
521	....	014	....
340	....	860	....

803	....	410	....
412	....	360	....
907	....	057	....
861	....	863	....
831	....	955	....
863	....	524	....
864	....	736	....
836	....	634	....
746	....	736	....
108	....	106	....
250	....	746	....
981	....	836	....
824	....	214	....
210	....	846	....
266	....	879	....
836	....	625	....
107	....	102	....
410	....	216	....
715	....	869	....
975	....	543	....
778	....	655	....
743	....	457	....
764	....	167	....
215	....	561	....
076	....	640	....
864	....	654	....
876	....	667	....
754	....	301	....
865	....	109	....
198	....	616	....
8636	....	7474	....
7874	....	7355	....

1177	....	1087	....
2276	....	2435	....
7425	....	8655	....
7654	....	6422	....
7776	....	6554	....
5432	....	6544	....
7656	....	5432	....
9879	....	8701	....
8611	....	0187	....
9870	....	0676	....
8765	....	3342	....
3776	....	2243	....
7543	....	7701	....
1073	....	7653	....
7653	....	7622	....
8763	....	5432	....
5324	.....,........	6542	....
6422	....	7055	....
0652	....	8764	....
8643	....	7654	....
6117	....	1153	....
7702	....	8673	....
5422	....	7533	....
8761	....	5733	....
8276	....	7373	....
7271	....	8861	....
0176	....	1760	....
8766	....	2344	....
7653	....	5432	....
6510	....	6530	....
1074	....	7119	....
9840	....	1105	....

7531	....	7401	....
8376	....	8764	....
1876	....	2876	....
1652	....	7654	....
1088	....	7601	....
6707	....	8754	....
8761	....	8110	....
3051	....	8765	....
2432	....	5492	....
7532	....	3346	....
6501	....	5443	....
8765	....	4455	....
7651	....	1877	....
1086	....	7550	....
8766	....	4466	....
8770	....	7701	....
8761	....	5420	....
1106	....	6243	....
4323	....	6421	....
9230	....	4429	....
5863	....	3327	....
6543	....	8761	....
9254	....	0185	....
1074	....	8242	....
7231	....	5530	....
1875	....	9872	....
9116	....	7049	....
5254	....	7285	....
2127	....	0423	....
4962	....	4671	....
6630	....	9014	....
7351	....	4185	....

3752	....	2753	....
8296	....	1172	....
9274	....	4827	....
5701	....	8566	....
3088	....	9862	....
2849	....	8421	....
76541	....	46532	....
75251	....	64321	....
19865	....	98010	....
44903	....	66254	....
37620	....	65432	....
95411	....	27548	....
95338	....	86421	....
15154	....	08435	....
85368	....	18642	....
36437	....	74322	....
47720	....	52740	....
76200	....	79284	....
51914	....	29476	....
68223	....	13654	....
01677	....	29370	....
82101	....	35726	....
44626	....	64651	....
50663	....	45609	....
27391	....	82546	....
99265	....	21419	....
56438	....	47538	....
14732	....	49762	....
38656	....	95078	....
63643	....	91636	....
30079	....	26090	....
17532	....	14160	....

98732	....	88572	....
17643	....	55621	....
49289	....	38247	....
79232	....	19376	....
82448	....	01753	....
28299	....	46517	....
57033	....	29645	....
49221	....	85321	....
70165	....	38585	....
93754	....	01763	....
01532	....	37479	....
92750	....	45072	....
62990	....	82643	....
15719	....	73152	....
93761	....	21814	....
07626	....	48211	....
50079	....	73760	....
49386	....	83742	....
94703	....	15228	....
95750	....	37542	....
17740	....	94666	....
28252	....	95470	....
48659	....	35438	....
94552	....	65221	....
01753	....	14702	....
72034	....	93225	....
83371	....	46013	....
83608	....	93972	....
26441	....	13286	....
48512	....	92035	....
95206	....	02561	....
84351	....	78246	....

16842	....	08221	....
93866	....	49652	....
84610	....	42982	....
12547	....	60257	....
62938	....	46103	....
47249	....	50251	....
52951	....	83703	....
07649	....	15732	....
29331	....	62968	....
345782	....	987103	....
201895	....	916845	....
456781	....	376519	....
569831	....	238754	....
387512	....	452875	....
984763	....	045017	....
298435	....	112784	....
090768	....	234742	....
954136	....	564219	....
759483	....	887631	....
656891	....	876925	....
332557	....	031409	....
476830	....	517194	....
219574	....	376489	....
857392	....	438752	....
386279	....	875315	....
619473	....	219563	....
219574	....	376981	....
487614	....	085376	....
764972	....	387519	....
114873	....	978563	....
576329	....	103865	....
657893	....	984371	....

349714 ....,.....	769102 ....
496510	041672 ....
392587	643191 ....
567681	638725 ....
284190	116793 ....
767935	436794 ....
432614	998664 ....
816154	654731 ....
764129	284937 ....
084502	563981 ....
278401	876943 ....
801018	932547 ....
342987	478901 ....
865013	543789 ....
987654	037685 ....
765839	258764 ....
965410	423698 ....
356793	175893 ....
763296	538721 ....
090807	443244 ....
578391	121376 ....
578342	987531 ....
013676	467831 ....
284679	538762 ....
998576	105789 ....
334876	857643 ....
876652	664892 ....
189567	356542 ....
987563	467357 ....
958746	465378 ....
836752	556793 ....
001578	567832 ....

378695	....	189695	....
276459	....	354672	....
287654	....	801567	....
765843	....	968476	....
310478	....	487103	....
875864	....	214376	....
468746	....	367529	....
954736	....	040472	....
657354	....	567830	....
951312	....	203916	....

CHAPTER THREE

READING PROBLEMS—A DISCUSSION

In this chapter I shall deal with subvocalisation, finger-pointing, regression, and back-skipping—areas that are major barriers to efficient reading. I shall include new approaches to both solutions and explanations, disagreeing strongly with much of what has been written before on these subjects.

Subvocalisation

A major reading problem is what is called 'subvocalisation', the tendency of a reader to 'mouth' the words he is reading. It is a product of the way in which children are taught to read: usually by the phonetic or phonic method or the look-say method.

The phonic method first introduces the child to the ordinary alphabet from a to z, and then introduces the various sounds of each letter so that 'a' can become 'ah', 'be' can become 'buh', and so on. The child is then introduced to the letters and sounds in the context of words. Thus 'the cat' will first be read 'tuh-huh-eh kuh-ah-tuh' (not see-aye-tee! etc.) until the teacher has moulded the word into its proper form. When the child has learned to make the correct sounds (vocalises properly) he is told to read silently. This last stage often takes a long time, and many children and even adults never get past the stage of moving their lips while reading. Those who *do* get past this stage may nevertheless still be vocalising *to themselves*. That is to say, as they read, they are consciously aware of the sound of each word. This is *subvocalisation*.

The look-say method of teaching children to read also relies on a word or verbal response. The child is shown a picture, for example a cow, with the word that represents the object printed clearly beneath it, thus: C O W. The teacher then asks the child for the correct response. If the incorrect answer is given (for example 'elephant'!) the teacher guides the child to the correct response and then moves on to the next word. It can be seen that when the child has reached a reasonable level of proficiency he will be in a position similar to the child who has been taught by the phonic method: able to read, still verbalising, and told that he should read silently.

These are of course only brief outlines, but they do help to illustrate that children who have completed their instruction in learning to read are left with the habit of vocally or subvocally repeating the words they are reading.

Virtually every book and course on speed reading maintains that this habit is one of the greatest barriers to improvement and that it *must* be overcome. It is my position that this attitude is only partly correct and that in many cases it can do more harm than good.

The truth of the matter is that subvocalisation does, undoubtedly, hold the reader back in certain circumstances, especially when he is dependent upon it for understanding. What must be added, however, is that in the real sense of the word subvocalisation *cannot* be completely eliminated. Once this is understood, the problem may be approached in its proper perspective, leading to much more satisfactory reading habits. People who are instructed to 'eliminate subvocalisation' often become discouraged and lose enjoyment in reading altogether after attempting for weeks to accomplish the impossible.

The proper approach to this problem is to accept that while subvocalisation *always* persists, it can be pushed farther and farther back into the 'semi-conscious'. In other words, while never being able to eliminate the habit completely, you can become less dependent upon it. Bearing this approach in mind, you need not worry when you occasionally realise that you are subvocalising, because it is a universal habit. What you should try to do is to become less dependent on this habit for complete understanding.

There is also a positive side to this habit which is seldom touched upon. One can actually use subvocalisation to *aid* the remembering of what has been read. Assuming that practice has enabled you to become less dependent on subvocalisation, you can consciously increase the 'volume' of subvocalisation when reading important words or concepts, thus making that bit of information stand out from the rest.

From now on, then, don't be as worried about this reading problem as others may have led you to be. Simply recognise it as a habit that everybody has in varying degrees, practise becoming less dependent on it by reading a little faster each time you read, and where appropriate use it to your own advantage!

Finger Pointing

Another area of great controversy is finger pointing. Most authorities consider it to be an extremely bad habit. Teachers in infant schools are continually faced with children whose finger is planted firmly under the words they are learning to read. Children seem to feel that with their finger serving as a pointer they can more easily guide their eyes to the part of the page they wish to read.

Many teachers discourage this, however, insisting that the child take his finger *off* the page and 'read properly'. Why? The answer is not clear. I have asked a number of teachers (and teachers of teachers!) and the answer usually given is that the finger 'slows the child down'. Now this may well be the case, if the child feels secure with his finger under a word and does not wish to move on to the *next* word. But it does not seem to be a very valid reply. For surely if the finger is placed on the book by the child because it helps his eyes, and if the teacher feels that the actual placing of the finger slows the child down, then the answer is *not* to tell the child to take his finger *off* the page, but to tell him to speed it up!!

If you happen to be a finger-pointer don't be perturbed—it is a natural habit and, if used properly, may lead to a great increase in reading efficiency. To begin with, you may find difficulty in speeding up your finger, because you will have become used to a certain rhythm and speed, but if you persevere solid gains should not be too far away.

Regression and Back-Skipping

Regression and back-skipping are so similar that they have been confused by many writers. The following distinction should help to place them in their proper perspective. *Regression* is a conscious returning to words, phrases or paragraphs

34

the reader feels he has missed or misunderstood. He feels he must return to them in order to understand the material. *Back-Skipping* is a kind of visual tic, an unconscious skipping back to words or phrases that have just been read. The reader is almost never aware that he is back-skipping.

As I explained in the last chapter on eye movements, back-skipping and regression add to the number of eye fixations per line, slowing down the reading process. Both of these habits are usually unnecessary. Studies performed in the conscious re-reading of material indicate that readers who were *sure* they needed to return to certain words or sections for understanding showed little change in comprehension scores when not allowed to do so. It is not so much a matter of comprehension as of confidence in your mind's ability.

My approach to eliminating or reducing these two habits is two-fold. Initially you must *force* yourself not to re-read sections you think you may have missed, and then you must gradually push up your speed, trying to maintain an even and flowing rhythm in your eye movements. Both speed and rhythm will make back-skipping and regression more difficult, while actually improving your comprehension.

The three problem areas: subvocalisation; finger pointing; and back-skipping and regression may now no longer be seen as the major barriers so many people have made them out to be. They are simply habits that can be overcome, and in some cases used to great advantage.

You are now ready to take your second Self Test. Since taking the first test you have learnt about eye movements and about the various problems many people have with reading. In this next test put your new knowledge to work; try to increase the length of each fixation and try to overcome whatever problems you have been having. *Consciously* push yourself a bit faster than you would normally read, while making every effort to comprehend what you are reading. When you have finished this exercise calculate your w.p.m. as before (in this article there are 1500 words), answer the questions that follow, calculate your comprehension and enter both scores on your progress graph.

From this point on in *all* your reading push yourself to go just that *little bit* faster.

INTRODUCTION TO PSYCHOLOGY

The Definition of Psychology

Psychology may be defined *as the science that studies the behaviour of man and other animals.* For this definition to be useful, it is necessary to specify more clearly what psychologists mean by behaviour. We can get some idea of what *behaviour* means to the psychologist if we look briefly at the topics covered by psychology:

1. *The behaving organism.* As a science rooted in biology, psychology is interested in the bodily processes that make activity possible. Thus psychologists often refer to the stimuli (singular stimulus) that impinge upon sense organs, and to the responses that occur because of the way the organism operates. Stimuli include the lights, sounds, odors, pin-pricks, and other physical energy sources that are the external (and sometimes internal) occasions for what the organism does, goading it to action, interrupting what it is doing, directing its choices. The responses (in man) are what he does when his brain is active, his muscles move, and his glands secrete. We therefore touch briefly on the operation of the *skeleton* and the *muscles*, moving on to glance at the varied functioning of the endocrine (ductless) glands, such as the thyroid or the sex glands. But psychologists are particularly interested in the *nervous system* and especially in the *central nervous system*, whose most complex portion is the *brain.*

It has been found, for example, that there are centers deep in the brain (in a part of the brain, old from an evolutionary standpoint, called the hypothalamus) that appear to produce the equivalent of pleasure or of pain when these centers are electrically stimulated (Olds and Olds, 1965). Psychologists not only participated in the original experiments in which this discovery was made, but have since carried out a number of further experiments to determine how similar the responses to electrical stimulation of the brain are to the effects of external pain or food reward. For example, studies have been made of the reaction to conflict whan a thirsty rat receives an electric shock as it attempts to drink. The rat at once approaches the water and withdraws from it in fear, assuming a characteristic posture. When the shock is received through an implanted electrode in the brain, the rat behaves just as if a shock had been received on its snout. Thus it appears plausible that the shock through the electrode is equivalent to painful stimulation.

2. *Growth and development.* The child is indeed 'father of the man.' We can understand much of adult behaviour only through a knowledge of the course of its development in the child. Two principles stand out as we study human development. One is that the growth of the body and the nervous system follows certain patterns rooted in biology. These are reflected in the concept of *maturation* of the organism along built-in (inherited) lines. The other is that a mature organism is also a product of *learning*. In man, this learning is in part a product of *social living*, a product of his *culture*. Hence in studying human development, we are interested in the processes of socialization, that is, the ways in which the infant turns into a civilized person.

3. *Motivation and emotion.* The newborn infant is aroused to activity by his bodily needs—the needs for air, food, elimination, a comfortable temperature, sleep. All such needs are the physiological roots of what psychologists call motivation. But motives become complex as the individual grows up, and psychologists study how they are acquired, how strong they are, and how people differ in their motives. Some individuals conform readily to their cultures, others rebel; some develop good work habits and have high motives to achieve, others are more shiftless; some are competitive and aggressive, others self-effacing. Emotions and motives are closely related, for the excitement of highly motivated activity has its emotional colouring; aggressive behaviour may be accompanied by deep feelings of anger, flight from danger by strong fear.

4. *Perception.* We perceive the world through our eyes or ears or by way of our other senses. But what is perception? How is it that we recognize a given colour as red, or hear one sound as music and another as noise, or 'sense' that one facial expression is friendly and another hostile? From its earliest days psychology has devoted a great deal of attention to such questions. It is clear that perception depends not only on our equipment of

sense organs, but also on the structures in our nervous system which enable us to say 'This is hot' or 'That tastes salty.'

We shall be concerned too with problems of consciousness. How does our physiological state when alert and awake differ from conditions of sleep? We shall see that there is no sharp distinction between conscious and unconscious states; rather there are degrees of awareness in which we may be more or less receptive to stimuli in the environment. Even during the stage of sleep where dreaming occurs we may be affected by events that take place around us.

5. *Learning and thinking.* Because of its importance learning is a topic of special interest to psychologists, both in its theoretical aspects and in its practical aspects. The theoretical problems of learning include the answers to such puzzling questions as how rewards and punishments operate; what goes on when we remember and when we forget, or when we acquire skills; how learning one thing affects the learning of others. The answers to these questions have important practical consequences, for much social effort goes into learning and teaching—of the young by parents and teachers, of apprentices on the job, of members of industrial and business organizations as they face new tasks.

A new interest in 'programmed' learning, often using so-called teaching machines, illustrates the practical consequences of experimental studies of learning. *A programme* is an attempt to apply what we know about the essential features of learning to the task of individual instruction, using a technique in which each step of the process is carefully planned to provide the best conditions for learning. We shall consider later on the detailed ways in which such programmes make use of learning theory; for the present we may merely indicate that there have been promising successes in their use. For example, it has been reported that elementary school children who studied their mathematics by using a programme presented by a computer-controlled teaching machine did much better than those who learned it in the conventional way (Suppes, 1967).

Thinking and problem-solving make use of what we have learned, and thereby provide the occasions for new learning. The interrelations between learning and thinking, including the role of language, furnish plenty of problems for investigation.

38

6. *Individuality and personality.* Individual uniqueness is a product of the hereditary and environmental influences that have shaped the person; the accidents of his birth and up-bringing, what he has perceived and learned, what he has thought about. Psychologists have developed various ways of assessing or measuring many kinds of differences among people. Perhaps the most familiar of these devices is the intelligence test.

But intelligence is only one aspect of individuality. All of us know people of whom we say 'He's a real person' (or, regrettably, 'He's got quite a personality'). What is personality? What is it that conclusively distinguishes one individual from another? And what do we mean when we speak of the 'self?' These are questions of much concern to psychology.

7. *Conflict, adjustment, and mental health.* For many readers, this aspect of psychology may seem the most important. How does a person meet frustration and conflict? What happens when he can no longer cope with his problems in ordinary ways? Is 'Adjustment' an ideal, or not? What, indeed, is mental health? While psychology has no final answers to these questions, it has at least been able to shed some light on them. There have been some successes in applying the methods of the experimental laboratory to these fields, and much has been accomplished in developing new techniques for treating mentally ill individuals.

8. *Social aspects of psychology.* The old saying; 'Two's company and three's a crowd,' familiar as it may seem in one context, illustrates a number of basic psychological questions. What is the difference between the response of an individual to his physical environment and his response to that same environment in the presence of another individual? What do we mean by a group, and how does group behaviour differ from and affect individual behaviour?

TEST 2 (1,400 words)

1. Psychology is the science devoted to the study of the behaviour of man only.   True   False
2. The science of psychology is rooted in biology.   True   False
3. The central nervous system is the most im-

portant part of the nervous system, and does not include the brain. True False

4. We cannot understand much of adult behaviour through a knowledge of its development in the child. True False

5. The two principles that stand out as we study human development are motivation and emotion. True False

6. Bodily needs are the psychological roots of emotion. True False

7. Emotions and motives are closely related. True False

8. Perception depends only on our sense organs. True False

9. Psychology has recently been able to make a sharp distinction between conscious and unconscious states. True False

10. The theoretical problems of learning include the answers to such questions as how rewards and punishments operate. True False

11. Programmed learning makes use of integration but does not yet use teaching machines. True False

12. Individual uniqueness is a product determined solely by heredity or genetic 'passing on'. True False

13. Intelligence is not really an aspect of individuality. True False

14. Psychology has a number of final answers to the question of mental health. True False

15. 'Two's company and three's a crowd' is quoted because it illustrates one basic psychological question. True False

CHAPTER FOUR

VOCABULARY (1)

Having dealt with our introductory material, the theory behind eye movements and the major problem areas in reading, we now move on to the first of three sections on vocabulary. This factor is generally considered to be the most important individual item in the development of efficient reading. It is perhaps not so surprising when one realises that the extent of one's vocabulary is an indication of the extent of one's knowledge, which in turn is an indication of the amount of material that one has been able to read.

Schools, colleges and universities include general vocabulary testing as one of the major criteria by which they judge the suitability of applicants, and the success or failure of a student often depends on his ability to understand and use words properly.

The importance of vocabulary extends, of course, far beyond the academic world: the businessman who has at his command a wider range of words than his peers is at an immediate advantage, and the person who, in social situations, can both understand easily and comment creatively also has the upper hand.

Before getting down to the practical side I should like to mention another important point. Most of us have more than one vocabulary. In fact we usually have no fewer than three. First is the vocabulary we use in *conversation*, and in many cases this may not exceed 1,000 words (it is estimated that in the English language there are well over 1,000,000 words!).

Our second vocabulary is the one we use when *writing*. This tends to be larger than the spoken one, because more time is devoted to the construction and content of sentences, and because there is less pressure on the writer.

The largest of our three vocabularies is our *recognition* vocabulary—the words that we understand and appreciate when we hear them in conversation or when we read them, but which we ourselves may not use either in writing or in conversation. Ideally, of course, both our speaking and our writing vocabularies should be as large as our recognition vocabulary, but in practice this is seldom the case. It is possible, however, to increase all three quite drastically.

The purpose of this chapter is to introduce to you over eighty prefixes (letters, syllables, or words placed at the commencement of a word). As our English language has a large element of Greek and Latin, you will note that many of the prefixes are taken from these two languages.

Study the following list thoroughly. A complete understanding of it will give you the key to thousands of unfamiliar words. In later chapters you will find a similar coverage of suffixes and roots.

Following the prefixes are three vocabulary exercises designed to give you practice with your new knowledge. These exercises are not vocabulary tests in the strict sense. In many cases definitions have been 'stretched' a little in order to include a key word that carries an appropriate prefix.

When doing this exercise break up each of the words from which you select, trying to establish its meaning from its structure. To help you with this, have a dictionary at hand.

When you have filled in each of the fifteen blank spaces with the letter of the word you think is correct, check your answers on page 157.

PREFIXES

Prefix	Meaning	Example
a-, an- (G)	without, not	amorphous
ab-, abs- (L)	away, from, apart	absent
ad-, ac-, af (L)	to, towards	advent, advance
aero-	air	aeroplane, aeronaut
amb-, ambi- (G)	both, around	ambiguous
amphi- (G)	both, around	amphitheatre
ante- (L)	before	antenatal
anti- (G)	against	antidote, antitoxic
apo-	away from	apostasy
arch- (G)	chief, most important	archbishop, archcriminal
auto- (G)	self	automatic, autocrat
be-	about, make	belittle, beguile, beset
bene- (L)	well, good	benediction

Prefix	Meaning	Example
bi- (G)	two	biennial, bicycle
by-, bye- (G)	added to	by ways, by-laws
cata- (G)	down	catalogue, cataract
centi-, cente- (L)	hundred	centigrade, centenary
circum- (L)	around	circumference, circumambient
co-, col-, com-, cor- con-, (L)	together with,	companion collect, co-operate
contra- (L)	against, counter	contradict, contraceptive
de- (F)	down,	denude, decentralise
deca-, deci (G)	ten	decade, decagon
demi- (L)	half	demigod
dia- (G)	through, between	diameter
dis- (L)	not, opposite to	dislike, disagree
duo- (G)	two	duologue, duplex
dys-	ill, hard	dysentry
e-, ex-	out of	exhale, excavate
ec- (L)	out of	eccentric
en-, in-, em-, im-, (L; G) (F)	into, not	enrage, inability, embolden, emulate, impress
equi-	equally	equidistant
epi- (G)	upon, at, in addition	epidemic, epidermis
extra- (L)	outside, beyond	extra-essential
for-, fore- (E)	before	foresee
hemi- (G)	half	hemisphere
hepta- (G)	seven	heptagon,
hexa- (G)	six	hexagon, hexateuch
homo- (L)	same	homonym
hyper- (G)	above, excessive	hypercritical, hypertrophy
il-	not	illegal, illogical
in-, im- (un) (L, G, F)	not	imperfect, inaccessible
inter- (L)	among, between	interrupt, intermarriage
intra-, intro- (L)	inside, within	intramural, introvert
iso- (G)	equal, same,	isobaric, isosceles
mal- (L)	bad, wrong	malfunction, malformed
meta- (G)	after, beyond	metabolism, metaphysical
mis-	wrongly	misfit, mislead
mono- (G)	one, single	monotonous, monocular
multi- (L)	many	multipurpose, multimillion
non-	not	nonsense, nonpareil
ob-, oc-, of-, op- (L)	in the way of, resistance	obstruct, obstacle, oppose
octa-, octo- (G)	eight	octahedron, octave
off-	away, apart	offset
out-	beyond	outnumber, outstanding
over-	above,	overhear, overcharge
para- (G)	aside, beyond	parable, paradox
penta- (G)	five	pentagon, pentateuch
per- (L)	through	perennial, peradventure
peri- (G)	around, about	perimeter, pericardium
poly- (G)	many	polygamy, polytechnic
post- (L)	after	postscript, postnatal

43

Prefix	Meaning	Example
pre- (L)	before	prehistoric, pre-war
prime-, primo- (L)	first, important	primary, Prime-Minister
pro- (L)	in front of, favouring	prologue, pro-British
quadri- (L)	four	quadriennial, quadrangle
re- (L)	again, back	reappear, recivilise
retro- (L)	backward	retrograde, retrospect
se-	aside	secede
self-	personalising	selfcontrol, selftaught
semi- (G)	half	semicircle, semidetached
sub- (L)	under	submarine, subterranean
super- (L)	above, over	superfluous, superior
syl-	with, together	syllogism
syn-, sym- (G)	together	sympathy, synchronise
tele- (G)	far, at or to a distance	telegram, telepathy
ter- (L)	three times	tercentenary
tetra- (G)	four	tetrahedron, tetralogy
trans- (L)	across, through	transatlantic, translate
tri- (L; G)	three	triangle, tripartite
ultra- (L)	beyond	ultramarine, ultra-violet
un- (im) (L, G, F)	not	unbroken, unbutton, unable
under-	below	underfed, underling
uni- (L)	one	unicellular, uniform
vice- (L)	in place of	viceroy, Vice-President
yester- (E)	preceding time	yesterday, yesteryear

Vocabulary 1(a)

1. .... is reserved for the most important and most dangerous of one's opponents.
2. A .... is a two-footed animal.
3. A person or thing beyond comparison, a model of excellence, is known as a ....
4. Streams that flow together are said to be ....
5. A coalition of three men for purposes of government or administration is called a ....
6. Many people in the world are not able to read; they are ....
7. .... is the introduction of one substance into another.
8. Because people estimated that this creature had 100 legs, they called it a ....
9. .... means third in rank, order, or succession.
10. One opposite of fascination is ....
11. To go against restrictions laid down is to .... the rules.

44

12. A creature that can live in both air and water is called an
....
13. .... means operating in a backward direction.
14. A .... is a person who speaks many languages.
15. If you have a strong feeling against something you are said
to be ....

a. polyglot   b. amphibian   c. disenchantment   d. centipede
e. biped   f. confluent   g. illiterate   h. antipathetic
i. retroactive   j. contravene   k. tertiary   l. archenemy
m. paragon   n. triumvirate   o. impregnation

Vocabulary 1 (b)
1. One who does not believe in God is an ....
2. He was a .... because he has a fixation on a
single subject.
3. The Ten Commandments are often called the ....
4. An outstanding object or person is said to be ....
5. A plane figure with eight sides and angles is known as an
....
6. To .... means to dig away the foundations, to
bring down from below.
7. A .... is a graveyard below ground.
8. A person who .... gives up a claim, resigns, gets
away from a situation.
9. An injection into the returning blood stream is called an
.... injection.
10. When something gets in the way of light or meaning, it is
said to ....
11. To consider one's self to be above others is to possess a
.... attitude.
12. The medical condition in which one loses one half of one's
field of vision is known as ....
13. A .... is an instrument that enables observers to
look over an object.
14. A line on a map which connects those places having equal
average temperature is called an ....
15. An .... is a person who writes his own life story.

45

a. intravenous   b. autobiographer   c. abdicates
d. Decalogue   e. atheist   f. undermine   g. supercilious
h. isotherm   i. monomaniac   j. octagon   k. catacomb
l. obfuscate   m. periscope   n. prominent   o. hemianopsia

Vocabulary 1 (c)

1. A dividing membrane between two areas is called a
   ....
2. .... applies to what is immaterial, incorporeal,
   supersensible, beyond the physical.
3. A .... is a curse.
4. To .... means to bring up or throw back from a
   deep place; to vomit.
5. A .... is someone who is of no importance.
6. An ancestor may also be called a ....
7. When something passes through, permeates, extends and
   is diffused, it is said to ....
8. If you ...., you are going beyond ordinary
   limits.
9. A verse containing five feet is called a ....
10. .... is charity, kindness or generosity.
11. If you are prudent and wary, and look all around before
    doing anything you are ....
12. Something capable of being calculated beforehand is
    ....
13. That which has existed from the beginning, we call
    ....
14. To .... means to subdue by superior force; to
    bring under the yoke.
15. If we interpret something wrongly, we .... it.

a. metaphysical   b. regurgitate   c. forebear   d. extravagate
e. misconstrue   f. primordial   g. circumspect   h. diaphragm
i. subjugate   j. predeterminable   k. nonentity   l. pentameter
m. beneficence   n. pervade   o. malediction

46

CHAPTER FIVE

CONCENTRATION, COMPREHENSION & CONDITIONS

Having tackled basic theory and basic problems, and having started to improve our word weaponry, we are now ready to discuss the concepts of concentration and comprehension and the physical conditions in which they can be maximised.

Concentration is most important if the reader is to get full value from the material he is reading. If you yourself have not experienced difficulty in this area, I am sure you will have heard people complaining that they just could not 'settle down' to the reading task at hand. In many cases even when they really wanted to read something they found themselves unable to do so.

The many causes for lack of concentration include vocabulary difficulties; conceptual difficulty of the material; inappropriate speed; incorrect mental approach or set; poor organisation; lack of interest; lack of motivation; wrong time for reading; poor health; interference; and poor reading conditions.

Vocabulary Difficulties

These have already been dealt with to some extent in the previous chapter. If the material being read continually confronts you with words which you do not understand or understand only vaguely, concentration will gradually become worse, because the ideas you are trying to absorb will be interrupted by gaps in understanding. A smooth inflow of information, unhampered by the lurking fear of misunderstanding, is a necessity for efficient reading. The vocabulary analyses and exercises in this book are designed to overcome this difficulty.

Conceptual Difficulty of the Material

This is a slightly more difficult problem to overcome and usually arises in study books. The best approach is to 'multiple read' the material. As this is one of the major problem areas in

47

all reading, I have devoted a special chapter, Chapter 13, to a very thorough analysis of it, attempting to provide a complete solution.

Inappropriate Reading Speed

This is often a product of the school system. When children are given important or difficult material, they are usually told: 'read this *slowly* and *carefully*'. This approach establishes a vicious circle, because the slower one reads the less one understands, which makes the material seem even more indigestible. Ultimately a point of complete frustration is reached and the material is often abandoned in despair! If you have difficulty with concentration and comprehension this may well be your trouble, so vary your speeds on problem material, trying to go faster rather than more slowly, and you may find a great improvement.

Incorrect Mental Approach or Set

This simply means that your mind has not really been directed in the best way toward the material you are trying to read. You may, for instance, still be concentrating on an argument that took place in the office, or a social engagement for the coming evening. What you must try to do is to 'shake out' the unnecessary threads that are running through your mind, directing yourself to think *actively* about the subject you are reading. You may even go so far as to stop for a moment and purposefully gather together your thoughts. As with multiple reading, I shall be examining the question of mental set in greater detail in the study chapter.

Poor Organisation

This is a far commoner sin than many realise. Actually getting down to reading a book is a problem of the will, and almost demands a run-up to the desk in order to gain enough impetus actually to sit down at it! Having arrived and started to read many people suddenly realise that they don't have a pencil, note-paper, their glasses and any number of other things, and consequently disrupt their concentration to get these materials. The solution is easy: before you sit down to read, make sure that all the materials you will need are readily available. Not just 'nearby' but *readily available*.

Lack of Interest

This is a problem most often experienced by students or people taking special courses. We devote special attention to it at the College of Advanced Reading. The first step in correcting this problem is to review the items I am discussing in this chapter, for lack of interest is often related to other difficulties: obviously interest, will be difficult to maintain if a deficient vocabulary is continually interrupting understanding, if the material is confusing, if other thoughts keep popping up, and if necessary materials are not available.

Assuming that these problems are overcome and that interest is still not as high as it should be, we must analyse the personal approach to the material. The first step is to make sure that the technique being used is appropriate, and here I once again refer you to the Buzan Study Technique chapter further on. If all this fails, the following approach has proved useful to those who have come to what they thought was 'the end of the line'. This approach makes you a 'Severe Critic'. Rather than reading the material as you normally would, get annoyed at it for having presented you with problems and try to analyse it thoroughly, concentrating even on the negative aspects. You will find yourself actually becoming interested in the material, much in the way you become interested in listening to the arguments of someone whom you don't particularly like and wish to oppose vigorously!

Lack of Motivation

This is a different problem, often stemming from having no clearly defined purpose. The solution follows the same approach as in solving the problem of lack of interest, but should this fail to work you must analyse your reasons for reading the book or article in the first place. Often such a close look will lead to realisations that were previously dormant and increase motivation and desire. Sometimes this close look will lead you to the conclusion that you need not read the book at all! If the reasons in this respect are valid then, indeed, there is no point in reading the book. I must warn here that this may become a habit for those few who like to take the easy way out—so beware!

Reading at the Wrong Time of Day

This often makes the difference between a complete understanding of what is being read and a complete failure to understand it. Because of habits formed in school many have never experimented with the time of day at which they do their best reading or learning. Such experimentation is vital, for we all have different peaks and slumps in this regard. Some find that they study best between five and nine in the morning! others find they can study only at night, and still others that periods in the late morning or early afternoon are best. If you suspect that timing may be the cause of your inability to concentrate and comprehend, experiment as soon as possible.

Poor Health

This is an obvious drawback to any sustained efficient mental activity, and if you are likely to be involved in an extensive reading or studying programme, you should do everything possible to make sure that your physical resources are adequate to the task. Even such minor illnesses as colds and headaches may make a difference in intellectual performance. If you tend to have such symptoms semi-chronically, ask your doctor for advice.

Interference

This may reach the point of infuriation, although some people welcome interference as an excuse to leave the task! Just as unknown words and difficult concepts break the flow of concentration and understanding, so do telephone calls, unnecessary breaks, loud noises, and lesser diversions like transistor radios, doodle-pads and other items of fidgety interest that often litter a desk. The rule here is simply to be strong-minded and make sure that when you are reading and studying *that* is what you are doing and nothing else.

Physical Conditions

These include placement and intensity of light, height of

chair and desk, distance of eyes from the reading material, availability of materials, and physical comfort.

The best light to study under is daylight, and where possible the desk or reading platform should be placed near a window. If this is not possible, and in times of the day when daylight is insufficient, light should come from behind the left shoulder, to avoid glare. Desk lamps can often cause eye strain if not placed properly. The intensity of the light should be such as to illuminate adequately the material being read, and should not be too bright. The person who huddles up to his bright light lamp which beams directly on his book should take note. In addition to the desk lamp, it is well to have subdued general illumination.

The height of both chair and desk are important: the chair should be preferably straight-backed allowing the back of the thighs to rest comfortably, while the feet are placed flat on the floor. A common desk height is 29–32".

The distance of the eyes from the reading material should be approximately 18", a natural distance if one sits properly as described. Keeping the reading material this far away makes it much easier for the eyes to focus on groups of words, and considerably lessens eye strain and the possibility of headaches from reading. To convince yourself of this, try looking at your forefinger when it is almost touching your nose and then look at your whole hand when it is about 18" away from you. You will notice a real physical strain in the former, and a considerable easing of that strain in the latter even though you are 'taking in' more.

I have already discussed the availability of materials and will add only that a properly organised desk is not only better for concentration and understanding, but can also be a psychological boost. Knowing that things are pleasingly and functionally placed increases the enjoyment and ease of the task at hand.

Last but not least, a request that you not make yourself too comfortable! Many people look for the most comfortable and inviting easy-chair in the house, pad it even further with soft cushions, place a footrest in front of it so that they can stretch out more comfortably, prepare a steaming cup of hot drink or open a couple of cans of beer, and then settle down for two hours of intensive work to find two hours later that they have been asleep throughout!

Ideally your chair should be neither too hard nor too soft, should have a straight back-rest (a sloping one causes bad posture and back-strain and makes proper note-taking uncomfortable) and should in general neither make you too relaxed nor too tense.

Having worked on basic vocabulary, and having improved the mental and physical conditions of your reading, try your skills on the next self Test: *The Human Brain and Nervous System*. As before, bring *all* your new knowledge to bear on the material and push yourself to your limit. Don't be discouraged if on certain tests your scores dip a little — a fluctuating progress is expected and quite normal.

SELF TEST 3
THE HUMAN BRAIN & NERVOUS SYSTEM

The human brain is three pounds of 'messy substance shut in a dark warm place'—a pinkish-gray mass, moist and rubbery to the touch, about the size of a softball. Shock-absorbing fluid cushions it against bumps, sharp blows and other impacts. It is wrapped in three membranes, including an extra-tough outer envelope, and sits snugly in a crate of bone.

The brain is perched like a flower on the top of a slender stalk which in a six-foot man is not quite a yard long. The top three inches of the stalk, a thick white cable of nerve fibres known as the brainstem, lies entirely within the skull and is partly buried by the bulging halves or hemispheres of the brain. The rest of the long stalk, the spinal cord, is a direct continuation of the cable outside the skull. It runs down through holes in the vertebrae of the spine and ends at the small of the back.

Many branches extend from the central stalk, like the roads that feed traffic in and out of a superhighway. From the right side of the spinal cord thirty-one nerves pass through special windows between the vertebrae to the right side of the body. The same number of nerves pass by similar routes to the left side of the body. Besides the spinal nerves, there are a dozen pairs of cranial nerves which arise from the brainstem in the skull. Thus, eighty-six nerves connect the brain and the rest of the body. Through their finest fibres they reach into the remotest places, and into every nook and cranny from the roots of hairs and teeth to the tips of the toes. This is the general structure of the nervous system.

The nervous system is made up of a large number of cells with long extensions or 'tendrils.' They come in assorted shapes—ovals, pyramids, bulbs, irregular blobs. The biggest have main bodies about two thousandths of an inch in diameter, and networks of fibers which may extend from a fraction of an inch to several feet. Under the microscope a single brain cell with its fibers may resemble the crown of a tree. Growing out from each branch are smaller branches, and from each of them comes a succession of smaller and smaller offshoots down to the most delicate twig. The brain contains some thirteen billion such cells, five times more than the total number of people in the world.

These units form masses of twisted fibers, a tangle which one investigator has called the 'cerebral jungle'. Until recently most investigators assumed that nerve fibers occupy fixed positions, or at least moved only as they grew, like the roots of plants. But new studies (at the University of Texas) indicate that brain tissue is far more active. As you read this sentence, fibers in your head are swaying like sea-weed swept by tides. Tentacles of protoplasm are slowly moving forward, retreating, swelling and shrinking, waving from side to side.

Some twenty-three hundred years ago Hippocrates discussed this organ in terms which still make sense today: 'And men ought to know that from nothing else but from the brain come joys, delights, laughter and sports, and sorrows, griefs, despondency and lamentations. And by the brain in a special manner we acquire wisdom and knowledge, and see and hear, and know what are foul and what are fair, what are bad and what are good, what are sweet and what unsavory. . . . By the brain we distinguish objects of relish and disrelish; and the same organ we become mad and delirious, and fears and terrors assail us, some by night and some by day.'

CONTROLS AND ADJUSTMENTS

What is the brain for? Judging by what we know today, it is the great organ of adjustment. It plays the basic biological role of keeping us adjusted to unpredictable events in the outside world, of preserving our identities in an environment of swift and ceaseless chemical change.

Parts of you are continually dying and being born again. Some three million of your red blood cells die every second. Or to look at it another way, three million red cells are born every second, because the body continuously calls up fresh reserves to keep the total count the same.

Similar processes take place throughout the body. Deposits of fat, which were once believed to serve as warehouses for storing food surpluses, are more like department stores during the Christmas rush. Your waistline may not change, but everything else does. Fat molecules are destroyed and replaced in a rapid round of biological activity. And the same thing goes for muscles, skin, tendons, blood vessels. Steady changes occur even in bones which seem to be the most inactive tissues of all. It has been estimated that every seven years or so the body negotiates a complete turnover of all its substance. In other words, your body does not contain a single one of the molecules that were 'you' seven years ago.

These facts, many of them determined by modern methods of following radioactive tracers in the tissues, were not known to earlier biologists. They conceived of the body as a machine. Food was fuel, and the energy of combustion kept the machine going. All this took place within tissues that had to be repaired from time to time as they wore out. Otherwise they were relatively firm and unchanging structures. When the body was active, of course, it needed extra energy but during rest metabolism practically ceased until the next spurt of activity. We know that the actual situation is far different: all organisms must work merely to exist.

Life is more like a whirlpool than a machine. There is nothing machinelike about the vortex formed when water spirals downward. An entirely new whirlpool comes into being every few seconds as the rotating centre replenishes itself from surrounding waters. But through it all the form does not change. The features of the vortex, the shape of the spinning funnel remain the same over long periods of time. The system maintains its identity and structure—and your body is also a vortex of matter in a continual state of change. Your brain keeps you alive by balancing the processes of birth and decay.

These basic reactions have top priority. Everything else either helps in carrying them out, or else waits its turn. We pay a high price when the balance of any vital process is upset. For example, sugar is one of the body's energy-providing substances and we must have just the right amount, no more and no less.

You are walking a biological tightrope between coma and convulsion, the possible results of relatively slight changes in blood sugar levels.

But the brain usually receives advance notice of impending trouble. It receives a steady flow of information about current sugar levels, and makes adjustments as effectively as a pilot guiding an airplane through a storm. If there is too much sugar, the excess is burned up and excreted. If there is too little, the liver is instructed to release the proper amount of reserve sugar. Notice what such control implies. The brain must 'know' the desired sugar level. It must go by similar standards in regulating breathing (you probably inhale and exhale seventeen to twenty times a minute) and heart-beat rates (about seventy times a minute), and in holding body temperature at 98.6 degrees Fahrenheit.

The brain must also be in constant communication with all parts of the body. Indeed, it turns out to be the headquarters of the most elaborate communications network ever devised. Its activities are the result of the combined and patterned activities of billions of nerve cells. A nerve cell is a living wire which produces and conducts rapid electrical impulses. It keeps itself 'loaded' and ready for action with the aid of a built-in battery which runs on an oxygen–sugar mixture and recharges automatically. It fires—that is, emits up to several hundred impulses a second—when triggering impulses reach it from sense organs or from other nerve cells.

These outside signals enter the body of the cell through special receiving fibers which are usually short, fine and highly branched. The cell also has a transmitting or 'exit' fiber which, as a rule, is relatively long and thick. Its receiving fibers make delicate contact with the transmitting fibers of fifty other nerve cells on the average; some cells make contact with more than a thousand others. Thus signals are relayed from cell to cell as they pass through the nervous system. The rate at which a signal travels depends on the diameter of the fiber conducting it, the thickest fibers being high-speed express routes.

The slenderest fibers, about 1/25,000 of an inch in diameter have speed limits of a foot a second or two thirds of a mile an hour. But in large-gauge fibers, which measure about ten times thicker, nerve impulses flash along at speeds up to 150 yards a second, a respectable 300 miles an hour. Thick fast fibers generally connect remote parts of the nervous system; thin slow fibres connect neighbouring regions. Thus, if a cell communicates with several other cells at varying distances, the messages all tend to arrive at about the same time. This means that widely scattered parts of the nervous system can be stimulated, inhibited or alerted at once—a distinct advantage in co-ordinating complex behaviour.

The brain uses this network to adjust us to the outside world. Generally speaking its operation can be divided into three parts:

1. it receives input in the form of messages from the sense organs;

2. it organizes the input on the basis of past experience, current events and future plans;

3. and it selects and produces an appropriate output, an action or series of actions.

1. The human brain weighs approximately 5 lbs.	True	False
2. The human brain is wrapped in three membranes.	True	False
3. The brain stem lies entirely within the skull.	True	False
4. The brain can be likened to a flower.	True	False
5. Besides the spinal nerves, there are a dozen pairs of cranial nerves which arise from the brain stem.	True	False
6. The 'tendrils' of the nervous system are of similar shape.	True	False
7. The brain contains twice as many cells as the total population of the world.	True	False
8. The nerve fibres of the brain occupy fixed positions.	True	False
9. Aristotle said 'and men ought to know that from nothing else but the brain come joys, delights, laughter and sports, and sorrows, griefs despondency and lamentation'.	True	False
10. The brain ranks second to the heart as the great organ of adjustment.	True	False
11. Every second three million red blood cells die.	True	False
12. The substances of the body completely change approximately once each year.	True	False
13. Early biologists saw the body as a machine.	True	False
14. A nerve cell keeps itself 'loaded' with the aid of a built-in battery which runs on an oxygen–sugar mixture.	True	False
15. The communication network in the body is used by the brain to adjust to the environment.	True	False

CHAPTER 6

SKIMMING AND SCANNING

With the introduction of skimming and scanning we come to
yet another area where there seems to be a considerable amount
of misunderstanding and misdirected debate. In order to clarify this situation I shall first define the two concepts, and shall
then discuss the various confusions. At the end of the chapter
are exercises which will help not only to explain the concept of
scanning but which will improve to some degree your scanning
facility.

Skimming can be defined as that process in which the eye
covers certain preselected sections of the material in order to
gain a *general overview* of that material. In scanning the eye
glances over material in order to find a *particular* piece of information.

Skimming is a more involved concept that scanning and is
similar to the previewing techniques that I shall be discussing
in later chapters. Its basic aim is to provide a skeleton on which
the meat of the material can subsequently be placed. We shall
be delving into the application of this process shortly.

Scanning is a more simple process that is usually applied
when one is looking up a word in a dictionary, a name or telephone number in the directory, or a particular piece of information in a text book or report. The concept is not a sophisticated one, and its application is fairly simple. All you have to
do is to make sure before you scan that you know the basic
lay-out of the material you are scanning. This enables you to
save the time that so many people spend hunting around in the
wrong sections for the information they desire.

Apart from the slight confusion some authors have over
which is which, the words themselves have become the centre
of a reading controversy among academicians, advanced reading schools, and authors. The basic disagreement revolves
around the very concept of reading itself.

Can skimming, as some authors have claimed, be equated

with reading, and vice-versa? My answer is a definite no! As I have already explained, skimming is simply selecting *parts* of the material to be read in order to gain an overview: the eye reads special little sections. This can in no way be considered to be reading the entire text.

Advanced reading schools like the College of Advanced Reading teach, under instructor supervision, methods of reading that enable the eye to take in large areas of print at one time while using some form of visual aid. *This* process can be defined as *reading* because the reader is taking in all the words on the page. It has been mistaken by many people to be simply a different form of skimming, whereas in fact it is a different form of reading.

The confusion arises from the fact that certain skimmers have refined their art to such an extent that their comprehension seems to indicate that they have indeed read all of the material, whereas in fact they have very cleverly selected the major points.

The situation is further confused by those who say that Advanced Reading methods using large areas of print are actually teaching people only to skim. This again is not the case, as both the physics of the eye movement and the approach to the information being absorbed are quite different in the separate cases.

It is impossible, in a book, to teach the large-print-area method of reading, as this method requires class participation and very skilled instructor supervision, so for the time being we will scan and skim to the best of our ability!

On the pages that follow are a series of number-scanning exercises. Each page contains rows of numbers. The first number in each row is repeated *somewhere* in that row, and it is your task to spot it as quickly as possible. Start timing yourself, and with a pencil in one hand quickly check off the number in the row which corresponds to the number in the left hand column. When you have done this, record your time at the bottom of the page.

The exercises get more difficult as they progress, because the numbers are increased in size and are also made more similar. If you can maintain the same time for each page you will have done exceptionally well!

27	92	73	27	56	28	38	76
45	76	87	45	32	85	40	83
37	86	84	59	37	63	27	41
51	84	32	67	85	93	51	43
58	65	32	74	38	58	91	57
62	54	27	69	62	34	21	95
76	63	76	53	27	31	62	54
95	67	43	26	95	61	50	53
66	78	66	43	26	28	87	64
10	95	01	54	10	65	32	71
94	87	94	43	41	65	43	26
33	87	65	34	28	38	46	33
41	23	41	76	54	38	91	43
27	54	83	27	65	88	37	64
17	11	19	76	48	18	45	17
84	54	31	76	35	84	32	58
36	76	23	54	68	20	36	14
24	53	24	56	78	94	23	12
12	67	54	21	89	43	47	12
56	87	56	43	24	76	51	43
77	86	34	25	61	77	43	27
19	87	65	19	23	47	57	32
28	28	51	67	34	28	48	42

60   Time ....

674	567	674	874	638	890	568
624	873	270	017	624	734	905
671	671	874	235	437	281	238
910	742	342	553	276	910	901
763	542	673	763	245	664	321
878	771	543	753	271	878	646
752	257	265	371	752	347	235
843	765	342	567	843	235	542
876	564	234	876	654	234	567
821	543	821	653	265	387	418
102	201	546	102	653	812	112
456	789	234	251	456	745	321
237	197	673	367	237	635	637
847	764	637	847	635	425	852
846	783	736	635	781	843	846
335	771	326	873	335	763	872
378	672	837	378	736	891	810
281	536	281	986	253	653	271
443	764	237	443	265	781	753
657	689	342	561	675	657	823

516	615	516	893	625	847	782
827	827	651	825	837	653	445
745	873	754	745	755	432	891
653	763	563	566	653	365	871
874	198	235	471	874	236	714
654	564	445	645	654	348	251
843	256	345	761	918	843	348
118	881	818	453	116	118	342
822	522	782	282	882	822	768
845	352	764	238	845	458	326
874	187	874	784	237	453	267
187	234	118	553	178	187	456
465	345	564	456	465	234	265
876	456	345	234	237	876	678
781	871	765	187	465	781	118
123	132	123	546	781	432	234
567	543	234	567	765	576	891
562	562	265	256	786	198	234
776	667	676	891	776	453	234
765	664	678	765	654	367	918

62   Time ....

572	256	762	572	527	653	862
782	278	872	782	433	574	276
330	303	430	330	030	764	332
319	193	391	193	319	491	339
445	545	554	445	675	465	234
354	543	334	354	345	554	435
213	231	123	213	331	112	238
435	543	334	554	434	435	534
221	112	221	321	121	212	124
736	673	376	376	673	763	736
241	241	412	214	412	240	112
567	765	567	675	657	577	651
021	210	021	102	110	201	121
227	727	772	272	722	277	227
646	664	646	661	464	446	466
189	189	918	891	981	198	819
771	117	771	717	711	171	177
926	629	962	626	966	369	926
202	022	020	202	220	210	201
356	365	563	356	765	536	635

Time ....

119	991	191	116	910	199	119
553	335	353	553	331	551	354
012	120	102	021	012	104	211
482	484	482	248	428	824	842
216	612	621	261	216	126	616
527	725	275	527	752	257	572
2434	4426	6578	6754	2345	2434	2343
7876	7875	7867	7876	4567	3425	1987
3456	3456	7819	5432	7689	4563	2345
5682	3246	5621	5682	7621	8732	1956
1894	1948	1894	4526	7632	7682	1672
2214	2241	5622	6782	2211	2214	4124
5462	5462	8726	5672	7889	6532	0013
6781	1985	6721	6781	7628	9652	1934
5672	6582	8726	6738	6257	5267	5672
1872	1836	1872	8726	7627	1826	7827
2001	1002	0011	2001	1673	1020	1029
2679	8766	8687	6546	6437	2679	7443
7554	8664	5378	8676	7554	7676	5434
0864	0864	8765	7554	8775	5441	1644

Time ....

7543	8755	8541	7543	8754	6533	7632
8765	8764	8655	8765	6543	4654	5421
1654	5781	8653	7653	8753	8753	1654
8761	8764	7653	8762	7654	8761	8764
7663	8765	8875	7864	8764	5544	7663
8511	8765	1186	7641	8511	1894	6331
8631	8641	9864	8631	8613	8763	7631
8632	8763	8632	8764	8763	5438	5421
9841	8643	9841	0751	8643	8763	8763
8856	8654	8764	8856	8866	8685	6884
8674	8674	7863	6542	8734	8773	8764
1764	8641	1874	1763	1764	1457	8764
7237	7328	8753	6523	8642	7237	1876
2765	2864	6196	2765	7876	6543	7551
1287	1876	7765	5431	8641	1277	1287
5621	1976	7531	8734	5621	1256	8761
1987	8652	1987	1978	1874	6424	8763
7832	8783	8642	7823	8753	8742	7832
8753	8743	4865	8754	8753	6876	8723
1870	0986	1764	1708	1870	1077	1863

Time ....

8645	9875	1765	7875	8645	8723	8632
5765	5765	1776	8765	8764	8735	6878
8763	8754	8763	8723	8753	1874	1763
8765	7643	8756	7863	8765	8752	8763
1202	1022	1021	1202	1201	1276	8742
1852	7867	1864	1852	3257	6553	3457
5433	8763	5689	5433	3478	2346	8725
9742	9467	3685	8765	8765	4777	9742
7975	8754	8764	8764	7975	6346	6842
8763	8741	1874	8763	8641	7643	6781
7341	7341	8765	4567	2346	8765	3468
8652	8543	8652	4567	7654	8764	2356
8756	8754	8754	8756	7335	2564	8763
8764	8764	5421	7533	7643	8764	8768
6532	6135	5643	6532	6785	3477	8642
3455	3457	3486	3455	5543	2345	7532
5671	6531	2357	5436	1764	5671	6733
3477	4571	7642	3477	7763	6437	7538
2469	7432	1986	2469	9852	4579	7523
5743	9842	3670	4571	5743	6743	3567

Time ....

7523	6886	3567	4678	3478	5427	7523
8642	3568	8764	4588	8642	7543	3468
8531	5688	4488	8531	0165	1087	4671
8640	8650	6751	5571	7644	1753	8640
7301	1851	7410	7632	7301	0175	3466
3468	8532	4681	8751	3468	7631	8642
2457	7641	8643	4676	2457	8763	2475
7531	8641	3568	7643	1035	7531	8633
1875	1733	0567	8753	1875	8641	7432
8743	7532	7632	5688	8743	8753	3467
8755	8755	8875	5689	9755	4581	9751
8736	8761	8736	7754	7447	3568	7351
3468	7643	8875	3468	8753	1765	8441
1751	1750	1751	1741	8726	8763	8741
1977	1191	1977	7919	9771	8761	7791
8754	6754	8754	8547	8457	8744	8755
7653	6753	7653	3567	3567	5763	5368
1974	1974	1964	9147	7491	1947	1749
7864	7878	1755	7846	7864	4687	8746
8643	8648	8763	3486	8347	8643	3477

67   Time ....

8454	8455	8676	8454	4587	4584	8765
1175	1184	1765	1751	1157	1175	7641
8643	8637	8643	8641	4386	4368	8765
6432	2346	6433	6542	6432	3425	5432
8753	5784	8753	8762	4753	8735	3568
5241	8361	5412	7651	5241	8654	5242
7645	7654	7645	4765	5476	4577	5647
8411	8114	8411	1841	8711	4561	4811
8746	8764	4677	6488	7654	6874	8746
2574	2675	2574	2745	7452	4527	4452
7170	7701	7110	7171	7101	7170	0701
8741	7841	1874	8741	7814	1478	1784
4784	4788	4784	8747	8754	4784	4788
7632	7632	7623	2376	6737	2373	3728
3451	3434	3451	3541	1435	1543	5134
7633	7663	7336	7763	6733	7633	7636
8735	7853	6537	8735	8753	3578	9357

Time...............

CHAPTER SEVEN

PARAGRAPH STRUCTURE

In the preceding chapter we discussed the process of skimming in which certain pre-selected sections of the material are covered in order to gain a general overview. In this chapter we shall discuss the structure of the paragraph, thus enabling you to put into practice your skimming techniques appropriately.

Paragraphs, although looking very similar on the page as separated groups of words, are in fact tremendously varied within themselves. They range from the explanatory, through the descriptive, to the linking type. I am going to cover a very few of these to give you a general idea of how they can be approached, and shall give some general tips on methods that can be used to get more out of the paragraphs you are reading.

Explanatory Paragraphs

Are those in which the writer has set out to explain a certain concept or point of view. They will generally be quite easy to recognise, and hopefully easy to understand. This type of paragraph tends to commence with a statement about what is to be explained, which is followed by a series of progressive steps to what we hope is a satisfactory conclusion. When coming across this type of paragraph you may rest reasonably assured that the first sentence or two will give you a general idea of what is going to be discussed, that the last sentence or two will contain the result or conclusion, and that the middle of the paragraph will contain details. Depending on your goal in reading, you will, in the initial skimming, be able to direct your attention appropriately.

Descriptive Paragraphs

Usually contain an expansion of ideas on a subject that has been introduced previously or at the very beginning of the paragraph. Such paragraphs usually embellish, and as such are often not as important as those that introduce main elements. Of course there are exceptions in which the description of objects is vital, but in such cases the reader is usually aware of this importance.

Linking Paragraphs

Are those which join others. As such they often contain key information, for they will summarise the contents of what has preceded and what follows. For example: 'The theory of evolution explained above will now be placed in the context of the latest developments in the field of biochemical genetic research'. In this brief sentence we have been given an extraordinary amount of information, information that gives us in capsule form the content of part of the material we are reading. Linking paragraphs, then, can be very useful as guides.

There are of course numerous other types of paragraph, but the three mentioned are among the most common. How can one make use of the structures of paragraphs and their placing in the text to improve one's reading efficiency?

Perhaps most important is to realise that in many articles the first few paragraphs and the last few contain most of the significant information, the middle paragraphs containing particulars. If the material you are reading is of this type, concentrate, when skimming, on these paragraphs.

Other writers 'clear their throats' at the beginning before getting down to the meat of their presentation which is contained in the third or fourth paragraphs, and it is these of course on which the reader should concentrate initially.

There are also two 'games' that one can play with the structure of paragraphs which help enormously in understanding and maintaining involvement.

The first of these is to make up, as you read, a memory word for the main theme and the secondary theme of each paragraph. This exercise forces you to remain involved with the material you are reading, making you think about the material as you read it. Your ultimate aim should be to develop the facility of selecting these words as you read without any pause or interruption to the flow of your reading.

The second of these paragraph 'games' is to relate, as you read through the paragraph, the first sentence to the remainder, asking yourself whether this is introductory, transitional, encompassing, or in some cases nothing to do with the words that follow it.

Before moving on to the previewing chapter read a number of different kinds of material to give yourself practice in the art of recognising different paragraph types.

CHAPTER EIGHT

PREVIEWING

We come, in this chapter, to a concept at which we have been hinting all along: previewing material before it is read. The purpose of the preview is to develop a structure into which the mind can more easily fit the smaller details of that structure.

The previewer can be likened to a reconnaisance scout who goes ahead of the military force to determine the lay of the land, the position of the enemy forces, and areas of tactical advantage, etc. It is easier for an army to manoeuver and operate in unknown territory if it has major reference points, and in the same way it is easier for the mind to attack or understand information once it has major landmarks to go by.

Previewing should be applied to whatever kind of material you are going to read, whether it be letters, reports, novels, or articles. It will in all cases speed up your overall reading and will improve your understanding because you will no longer be stumbling over items one after the other, but will be fitting pieces into a general picture.

Your approach to the preview should combine the elements that I mentioned in the chapters on skimming and paragraph structure. In other words, you will sensibly and rapidly go over the material you are about to read, selecting those areas most likely to hold the major chunks of information.

The concept of previewing as described here is for use in your general reading. A more specific kind of preview will be discussed in the study chapter.

Your fourth Self Test, on The Major Musical Instruments, should mark a significant change in the way you read this kind of material. The previous chapters on Skimming and Scanning, Paragraph Structure and Previewing, combined with your experience of the perception exercise and pushing up your speed, should enable you to tackle this reading task with a considerable degree of sophistication.

Before you get down to the main reading, *preview* this passage as suggested. When you are in the process of reading it, apply all the techniques you have learned, and as before push yourself to the limit of your ability, attempting to improve on your previous Self Test performances.

SELF TEST 4
THE MAJOR MUSICAL INSTRUMENTS

The String Family

Nowadays, when we refer to the *strings*, we have in mind the violin family, consisting of four members—namely, the violin, the viola, the violoncello and the contra- or double-bass. These have many similar characteristics, but one of the chief differences is their size, ranging from the violin (the smallest), playing the highest notes, to the double-bass (the largest), playing the lowest notes. On all these instruments the strings are set in vibration with a bow, but sometimes the strings are plucked with the fingers. As the quantity of tone is not as great from stringed instruments as from wind instruments, many more string players than wind players are required in an orchestra. In a large symphony orchestra there might be as many as eighteen first violins, sixteen second violins, twelve violoncelli, and eight double-basses.

The shape of the violin, as we know it today, emerged during the middle of the 16th century, in Italy, having been gradually evolved from the rebec, a small bowed instrument of medieval times. The name *violin* was applied to all the members of this family, and not to the smallest one only. Louis XIV had a band of 'Twenty-four Violins' at his Court, and Charles II, on his return in 1660, set up a similar band in England. From this time the violin as such gained prestige in England, and the popularity of the viol gradually waned.

Plucked Instruments

It seems that the harp had its origin in prehistoric times, and might have come from the stretched string of an archer's bow, other strings of varying length (and pitch) being added, much in the same way as reeds or whistles were bound together to make a *syrinx* or pan pipes. The earliest evidence of a harp comes from Egypt and dates from the 13th century B.C.

73

The Harpsichord Family

The harpsichord was the most important of the keyboard instruments during the 16th, 17th and 18th centuries, holding a position analogous to that of the pianoforte of today. Three distinct instruments belong to the harpsichord family: *the virginal* (or *virginals*), the *spinet*, and the *harpsichord* proper.

Fundamentally they are all harps placed horizontally, with their strings plucked by plectra operated from a keyboard.

Other major stringed instruments include the lute, the mandoline and the guitar. Those stringed instruments which are hit include the piano and the clavichord.

Wind Instruments

All wind instruments are made to sound by causing air to vibrate inside a hollow tube. Part of this tube must be open, so that the air inside the tube has contact with the surrounding air. The inside of the instrument, known as the bore, may be cylindrical (the same width throughout its length) or conical (small at one end and gradually increasing in width to the other), or it may be cylindrical for part of its length and conical for the remainder. The hollow tube may be straight or curved.

The choice of material for a wind instrument depends on a number of factors, such as its ability to stand the strain imposed on it during the various processes of its manufacture, its durability, its capacity for being bent or coiled, and its weight. The instrument when finished must be hard and rigid and the inside of the tube must be smooth.

Wind instruments were played in very ancient times. In fact, remains of bone flutes of the Later Stone Age have been found. We know from the Bible that the flute was played in Hebrew religious processions, with drums, tambourines and cymbals, and a ram's horn was blown on special occasions.

Over 3,000 years ago the Egyptians used trumpets on ceremonial occasions and later the Greeks, at the Pythian games, were holding contests for solo playing on the aulos, a double-reed instrument, related to the oboe. The Romans, too, had a kind of oboe, and tubas of different sizes.

Since early times wind instruments have been gradually modified and improved and the orchestral instruments of today are almost as perfect as they can be for our present needs; but there is no knowing what further changes might be made, if, for instance, composers were to demand instruments with quarter-tones.

Wood-wind and Brass

Wind instruments are divided into two classes, the *wood-wind* and the *brass*. The term *wood-wind* does not signify that all the instruments in this class are made of wood; in fact, some are of ivory, of metal and of ebonite. Nor does the term *brass* mean that all these instruments are made of brass; there are some of silver, of copper, horn, ivory—and even wood!

The families of instruments generally regarded as wood-wind are: Flute, Oboe, Clarinet, Saxophone, Bassoon. The brass instruments are: Horns, Trumpets, Cornets, Trombones, Tubas.

This classification is based on the method of production of the sound. No sound will be made by simply blowing through the tube: a generator must be used. There are three types of generators: the *free air-reed*, the *cane-reed* and the *lip-reed*.

If the sound is generated by *air-reeds*, as in the flute, or *cane-reeds*, as in the oboe or clarinet, the instrument is wood-wind.

If the sound is generated by the vibration of the lips against a cup- or conical-shaped mouth-piece, the instrument is brass.

Percussion Instruments

Percussion instruments are members of an ancient instrumental family—perhaps the oldest. Some of its members still retain their primitive form in the modern orchestra.

Instruments of percussion have always been popular in Asia and Africa, and instruments from these continents have found their way into Europe at three different periods in history. It seems that during the 12th, 13th and 14th centuries the Crusades were responsible for bringing the kettle-drums (then called nakers) to Europe. During the 18th century the popularity of 'Turkish music' in European armies introduced via Austro-Hungary, caused the addition of a variety of percussive instruments. From the First World War, with the influence of American-negro music on dance-music, further additions have been made. The percussion instruments include the drum family, the triangle, the cymbals and the gong, all of which have no definite pitch; and the tubular bells, the celesta, the glockenspiel, and the xylophone.

The Organ

The organ is said to have originated in Chaldea and Greece, where it first appeared as Pan Pipes or Syrinx. Reeds were cut off just below the knot, so that air blown down the reeds had to return to the open end. These were therefore stopped producing a note nearly an octave below that produced on an open pipe.

By making a slit in the knot, and a notch with a bevelled edge in the pipe just above the knot, a sound could be made by blowing through the lower end of the reed. Thus the whistle-form of open pipe came into being.

The reed pipe, although used in bagpipes in ancient times, was not used in the organ until the 15th century.

The whistle pipes were placed on a wooden box, the wind-chest, and the wind was supplied by two people who blew through flexible tubes. Unless the pipes were stopped by the players hands or fingers, all the pipes sounded together.

The slider was next introduced. Each pipe was governed by a slider which was perforated, so that, on being drawn in or out, the wind to the pipe could be admitted or excluded. Next came a leather bag as a reservoir for the air, and later primitive forge bellows were used.

The Roman Hydraulus or water-organ came into being during the 3rd century B.C. By using the weight of water, the wind-supply system produced equal wind-pressure in the reservoir. Pipes were made of bronze and copper. There is evidence of a water organ which was in use during the 1st century B.C. It had one and a half octaves, with keys and three ranks of pipes, and produced 'Four-foot' pitch.

The organ was used for public feasts, and was not adopted for use in the Church until A.D. 450, when it was apparently used in Spain. In the 7th century it was used in Rome to improve the singing of the congregation. The art of organ-making was known in England in the 8th century. In the 10th century there was a large organ at Abingdon Abbey and another at

Glastonbury. Winchester Cathedral had a famous organ of 400 pipes of brass and copper. There were two organists; probably one worked the levers to make the pipes sound, while the other worked the stop slides. Only one key at a time would have been used. The keys were three inches wide, and the organist was known as *pulsator-organum* ('organ-beater').

By the 14th century fixed organs came to be called *positif* or *positive*, in contrast to *portative* (portable) organs, which were, by this date, being used in processions in Germany and Italy. The keys were closer together by this time, and could be operated by the fingers of the player.

By the end of the 15th century the organ was developing into its modern form, with two manuals and a pedal-board. By the 16th century pipes of conical construction were in use, and the keys were small enough for an octave to be spanned by the player's hand.

During the 18th century, Jordan, an Englishman, enclosed a section of the organ in a box with a sliding front, thus allowing the tone to swell or diminish, hence the term 'swell-organ'.

A marked development in the mechanism of the organ was made during the 19th century, whereby 'composition pedals', worked by the foot, enabled selected and fixed combinations of stops to be drawn.

By developing the use of the pneumatic lever for operating heavy mechanism, the use of larger organs was made possible. More recently electric mechanisms have replaced the mechanical type, giving greater control with less effort, allowing the organist to concentrate on the musical effect.

Since 1930 the electronic organ has been in use; this has neither pipes nor wind, and it is claimed that by electrical production many tone-qualities can be produced at will. It occupies no more room than a grand piano, and is considerably cheaper than a pipe organ; its installation requires little more than its connection to an electric power plug. The popularity of the pipe organ, however, seems to have been little affected by the electronic organ.

1. One of the chief differences in the string
   family is the relative size of the instruments.   True   False
2. There are more string players than wind
   players in an orchestra because the quantity
   of tone is not as great from stringed instruments.   True   False
3. The shape of the violin evolved from the
   viol.   True   False
4. When drawing-room music was the fashion
   a man of taste would often play the harp
   accompanied by his daughter or sister on
   the flute.   True   False
5. The earliest evidence of a harp comes from
   Egypt.   True   False
6. The virginal, spinet and harpsichord are
   basically harps.   True   False
7. *All* wind instruments are made to sound by
   causing air to vibrate inside a hollow tube.   True   False
8. In wind instruments the tube must be
   closed.   True   False
9. Wind instruments were developed after the
   Later Stone Age.   True   False
10. The instruments generally regarded as
    wood-wind are clarinet, saxophone, bas-
    soon, oboe, and flute.   True   False
11. Classification into wind and brass is based
    on the material used in producing the in-
    strument.   True   False
12. An instrument is brass if its unit volume is
    louder than that of wood-wind instruments.   True   False
13. The Crusades were responsible for bringing
    kettle drums to Europe.   True   False
14. The Roman Hydraulus was a famous Roman
    musician.   True   False
15. The organ was adopted for use in the
    Church in A.D. 250.   True   False

CHAPTER NINE

NEWSPAPERS

Newspapers are so much a part of our everyday life that we seldom stop to think that they are a very recent development. Prior to the 20th century the voice of journalism was virtually non-existent so far as mass audiences were concerned. Newspapers were in the main news-sheets with very little interpretive analysis or editorial comment. There was however one note-worthy exception: *The Times*, whose critical reports of the Crimean War in 1855 have been cited as influential in the downfall of the Cabinet and the army reorganisation.

It is interesting to note that the four oldest publications surviving the upheavals of history are not more than two hundred years old:

1. Berlingske Tidende   Denmark   founded 1749
2. Yorkshire Post   England   founded 1754
3. Neue Zürcher Zeitung   Switzerland founded 1780
4. The Times   England   founded 1785

The 19th century saw a steady growth of the world press, stimulated by the introduction of the Foudrinier machine which produced paper in an endless sheet. Parallel to this development was the universal growth of communication networks and education: more information was required more rapidly, and more people were able to read. As a result many of the world's newspapers were founded between 1840 and 1900.

In the early 20th century newspapers flourished, but even now, after a fairly short existence, many are entering more difficult times. One reason may be the spread of television, which in many cases can give a more immediate and personal coverage of a news event.

In the western world we may well be entering a stage in which the newspaper will change its function, dealing less with immediate news and more with summaries, analyses, and comment.

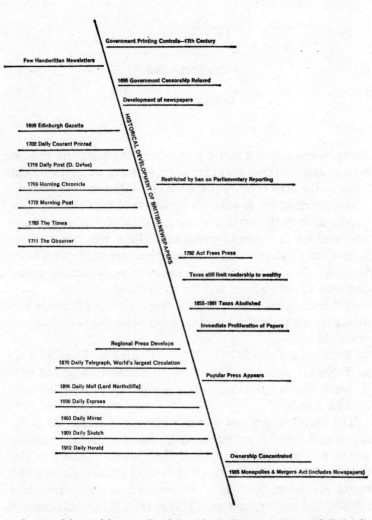

Government Printing Controls—17th Century

Few Handwritten Newsletters

1695 Government Censorship Relaxed

Development of newspapers

1699 Edinburgh Gazette

1702 Daily Courant Printed

1719 Daily Post (D. Defoe)

1769 Morning Chronicle

Restricted by ban on Parliamentary Reporting

1772 Morning Post

1785 The Times

1711 The Observer

HISTORICAL DEVELOPMENT OF BRITISH NEWSPAPERS

1792 Act Frees Press

Taxes still limit readership to wealthy

1855–1861 Taxes Abolished

Immediate Proliferation of Papers

Regional Press Develops

1870 Daily Telegraph, World's largest Circulation

Popular Press Appears

1896 Daily Mail (Lord Northcliffe)

1900 Daily Express

1903 Daily Mirror

1909 Daily Sketch

1912 Daily Herald

Ownership Concentrated

1965 Monopolies & Mergers Act (includes Newspapers)

A graphic guide to the historical development of British newspapers is included on the preceding page. The most recent collapses and mergers add interest to this overall picture.

Lest we become too concerned with our own press it is worth-while to take a quick look around the world at the circulation and influence of newspapers other than our own. The picture is astounding, if not a little disturbing!

1. *Asahi Shimbun* of Tokyo. Circulation 9,000,000 copies per day. This paper is not simply a popular daily; it exerts an enormous social and political influence.

2. *Izvestia*. Circulation 8,000,000 copies per day.

3. *Komsomolskaya Pravda*. Circulation 7,000,000 copies per day. Both *Izvestia* and *Pravda* are read by many more millions of people than the circulation figures show, being distributed throughout the entire Communist world, especially to the Communist leadership. These papers present a comprehensive picture of the Communists' view of their activity in all national and international spheres, as well as their view on matters connected with education, athletics, entertainment, and general philosophy. It has been suggested that these papers actually reach *hundreds* of millions of people.

4. *Jen Minh Jih Pao* of Peking. Circulation 2,500,000 copies per day. Although this circulation figure is not so high as the others already mentioned, this newspaper in fact probably reaches more people than any other journal in the world. It is the channel of state information for China, and is read out over the radio, on the trains, and on the factories and farms. Copies are also placed in glass-enclosed holders at intersections and market places.

5. *The New York Times*. Circulation 1,000,000 copies per day. Once again the circulation figures here are misleading, for this newspaper is read mainly by the leading economic, political, and communication communities in America and much of the Western World. Its influence on opinion-leaders throughout the world is enormous.

As a matter of fact the vast majority of the world's quality press seldom exceeds a daily circulation of 400,000 copies, and this includes three of the world's most educative and analytical newspapers: *Neue Zürcher Zeitung* of Switzerland, *The Times*, of England and *Le Monde* of France. As with *Jih Pao* and *The New York Times*, the circulation figures can be somewhat misleading in these cases, for the influence of these newspapers is considerable.

Having viewed newspapers in their international and historical setting, let us discuss briefly approaches to reading them. First, it is most important to have an organised approach. Many people spend hours reading their newspaper and come away feeling no more enlightened than when they began.

Whatever newspaper you read, it is always helpful to decide beforehand exactly what your aim is. To assist you in this decision always rapidly preview the newspaper before you read it, selecting the various passages and articles that you wish to read more thoroughly. Take a note also of the lay-out and typography, for pre-knowledge of where articles are continued, etc. saves a lot of page turning and fumbling.

Another point is that most people have a tendency to buy a newspaper which supports their general views—in other words they give themselves a little pat on the back every morning or evening! It can be a most interesting exercise to buy a different newspaper each day for a week, comparing and contrasting the layouts, the political bias, the approach of the reporters, the interpretation of news events, and the extent of the coverage. Try this during the coming week.

Another significant point is that newspaper reports should never be taken as gospel—I am sure that those of you who have been involved in a function or event which was reported the next day have often thought 'that's *nothing* like what happened at all!'

News is written by people who are likely to be biased or to be following a 'policy'. This 'misreporting', if we can call it that, is not necessarily intentional. Each person tends to see any given situation in a slightly different light.

Newspaper reporters are individuals, and they may even be seeing a given event from different physical locations (being in the middle of a stampeding crowd and being in a building watching that crowd stampede are bound to produce different reports.).

Accepting this basic and inevitable bias, we move on to the reporting of the event itself. The journalist will take down brief notes of what he wishes to report, will spend time travelling back to his typewriter, and will then reconstruct in his mind's eye the events that have taken place. Once again there will be slight and inevitable changes in emphasis which will be embellished by the words used to convey the situation.

Once the report has been written it has to be edited, and then re-edited before finally reaching the pages of the newspaper.

It can be seen that even with the most sincere of intentions, a *completely* objective report is almost impossible. Newspapers, magazines and journals should therefore be read with a far more critical eye than they usually are and what they report should be checked by news from other sources such as radio, television, and other journals.

This critical approach to reading involves analytical awareness and logical thinking. Still bearing in mind all that we have said on newspapers we now move on to the next chapter where more intricate details of analysis will be covered.

CHAPTER TEN

LOGIC

In this chapter a number of situations in which critical reading and thinking should be applied will be introduced. Items to be looked for and the readers' approach will be discussed in detail.

1. *Appeal to Authority*

In order to convince someone of the correctness or validity of a point, people often link their statements to an authoritative figure. For example 'Bob Boot, England's top football player, uses Tuff Nuff razor blades'. This linking with an authority automatically infers that the thing linked with is, in some way, as good as the authority itself. In reality the statement gives no pertinent or interesting information about the quality of the blades at all! This kind of argument is often used in advertising.

On a more sophisticated level such an argument may appear in a form like the following, where the authority quoted *does* in fact have some relation to the linked item: 'Plato, Aristotle, Kant and Bertrand Russell all agreed on the philosophical point that I am making'. This argument sounds strong, but as in the previous fallacy its weakness lies in the fact that the *statement* itself requires consideration rather than its supporters. It is perfectly possible that each of the famous philosophers mentioned as supporting a philosophical position could have made the same mistake!

In summary then, it is the *argument* and *not* the *man* which should be the basis for reaching conclusions.

2. *Denigration*

This is similar to Appeal to Authority, but in an opposite sense. The opponent of an idea will attack, instead of the idea, the personality of the people who are proposing that idea. The objection to this kind of argument is similar to that in Appeal to Authority: the man is not important; it is the argument itself that must be considered.

3. *Emotive Language*

This concerns the use of emotionally loaded words to cloud or distort judgment, preventing lucid examination of the arguments themselves. I remember well a Canadian newspaper headline which read: 'Canadian War Hero Traded for Commie Spy'. While reading the article I was expecting something far different from what the facts turned out to be: namely that the two men had been in identical positions, had very similar backgrounds, and had been caught by the respective countries in very similar circumstances. In other words a Canadian spy had been traded for a Russian spy!

Newspapers are often guilty of misleading language of this sort, and even the form of addressing notable persons may have very different associations. Think for example of the different reaction you get from a headline which starts: 'Mr. Heath . . .' and from a headline which starts: 'Ted . . .'

4. *Undefined Source*

Many reports include phrases such as 'usually reliable sources report', 'it has been confirmed that', and 'it is a commonly known fact that'. Phrases such as these should immediately alert the reader, for they are often substitutes for saying 'there has been a rumour that' or 'we are not really sure, but'.

This same fallacy often occurs in conversations that start with some such phrase as 'we all know' or 'everybody agrees'. But *do* we all know? And *does* everybody agree? Very often not!

5. *Extrapolation*

Extrapolation means that we decide, on the basis of information presently available, what will happen in the future or in different circumstances. This is a necessary process for helping us to make decisions, but it must be understood by those making the decision that extrapolating or predicting in this manner *never* leads to certainty, only to a probability. Many many mistakes are made because people are not aware of this, especially in economics and politics. How often have economic forecasts which were given almost as gospel gone completely awry because some important factor was not properly considered, or because an unforeseeable event loomed up just after the predictions were made.

The 1970 English pre-election opinion polls provide one of the best examples of this kind of fallacy. Even with enormous staffs, political experts and competent statisticians, most of the Poll Organisations were totally wrong in predicting a Labour Party victory.

Remember then, that extrapolation or predictive argument can be useful but never certain, and that anyone who says 'these things have happened and therefore this *will* happen' is treading on very slippery ground.

6. *Argument by Analogy*

An argument by analogy is one in which B is said to be like A and therefore a sub-section of B must be like a sub-section of A. This kind of argument can appear very convincing until one realises that if B is only *like* A, then in some ways it must be different! And arguments by analogy often fall down on exactly this point. i.e. the point which makes B *different* from A.

This kind of mistake is often made in analysing war situations, in which a present war is compared to a former war, all the similarities being trotted out as evidence that what we did or did not do then we should or should not do now. The differences are often left unconsidered and it is these (different equipment, different pressures of public opinion etc.) which are in many cases the most important factors. Whole theories of historical and economic 'cycles' have been elaborated on this basis, but while they may have a limited usefulness, they are seldom reliable.

Argument by analogy is often used in conversational discussion when people casually flip off statements to the effect 'well, such and such is like that, so the following *must* be true'. The 'following', as we have seen, need *not*, necessarily be true.

This is an insidious form of argument, so be on the look-out!

7. *Misuse of Statistics*

People often say 'you can prove anything by statistics'. What they are saying in effect is that if a person is not aware of all the considerations that go into a statistical statement, he can be easily mislead.

Let me give two examples of common misrepresentations which will indicate how statistics can be juggled.

The first is the fallacy of the 'average'. In this form of statement items are added together, and the total number is then divided by the number of items. Popular surveys often make this kind of error when they conclude that the average person feels a certain way about a certain topic. To illustrate just how wrong this kind of statement can be let us construct an hypothetical situation in which a country is almost at civil war over a moral question. If we assign numbers from one to a hundred for the strength with which a person aligns himself with one of the sides, we find that half the country is *completely* opposed, each person having a score of zero, while the other half is *completely* in favour, each person having a score of one hundred. A naive analysis of these statistics might lead someone to say that the average person in the country we are discussing scored fifty, which is representative of someone who does not really care.

In fact, as we have demonstrated, there is *no* average person in our make-up country, and half the population is ready to leap at the throats of the other half!

A second statistical misrepresentation is graphic. The shape and dimensions of graphs are changed to make the same situation look quite different. Rather than explaining this in detail I have included two graphs which show a progress during a ten year period. You will see how different they appear.

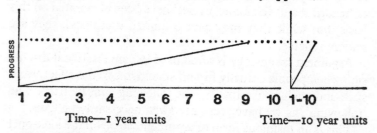

Time—1 year units   Time—10 year units

There are of course other logical fallacies, but the ones covered here are among the most important, and continually arise in newspapers and magazines as well as in mass media reporting and comment. They tend to arise similarly in conversation, and hunting them out can be a challenging and rewarding experience.

Near the end of Chapter 9 it was recommended that you read a number of different newspapers, bringing to bear on them all your critical abilities. Now that you have more weaponry, go quickly through them again noting in just how many places the various fallacies arise. To begin with you will find that hunting them down is a little difficult, but as you persevere your facility will increase considerably and your reading will not only be more enjoyable but will be more useful because you will have become a sifter rather than a sponge!

CHAPTER ELEVEN

VOCABULARY (2)

In Chapter 4 we discussed vocabulary in general, mentioning the tremendous importance it plays in reading efficiency, and the emphasis that is placed on it by educational institutions.

The fact that we have three different vocabularies, recognition, writing and speaking, was also covered and it was stressed that each of these three should be improved. At the end of the chapter I introduced you to over eighty prefixes which were then tested.

I imagine that by now your facility with this building block of vocabulary has increased considerably and that you will be ready for the next step in vocabulary building which is to learn the suffixes (letters, syllables, or words placed at the end of a word). As in the section on prefixes you will notice that most suffixes are taken from the Latin and the Greek.

Following the list of over fifty suffixes you will find a number of vocabulary tests similar to those you did in Chapter 4. As it is not possible, in the space of this book, for me to give you as comprehensive a test as I would like, I recommend that after having learnt the suffixes and completed the vocabulary tests to your satisfaction, you browse through a good dictionary, studying the various ways in which these suffixes are used. Keep a record of exceptionally good examples or examples which you find interesting and useful.

SUFFIXES

Suffix	Meaning	Example
-able, -ible (L)	capable of, fit for	durable, comprehensible
-acy (L; G)	state or quality of	accuracy
-age (L)	action or state of	breakage
-al, -ial (L)	relating to	abdominal
-an (ane, ian) (L)	the nature of	Grecian, African
-ance, ence	quality or action of	insurance, corpulence
-ant (L)	forming adjectives of quality, nouns signifying a personal agent or something producing an effect	defiant, servant

Suffix	Meaning	Example
-atable (L)	See -able, -ible	
-arium, -orium (L)	place for	aquarium, auditorium
-ary (L)	place for, dealing with	seminary, dictionary
-ate (L)	cause to be, office of	animate, magistrate
-ation, -ition (L)	action or state of	condition, dilapidation
-cle, -icle (L)	diminutive	icicle
-dom (E)	condition or control	kingdom
-en (E)	small	mitten
-en (E)	quality	golden, broken
-er (E)	belonging to	farmer, New Yorker
-ess (E)	feminine suffix	hostess, waitress
-et, ette (L)	small	puppet, marionette
-ferous (L)	producing	coniferous
-ful (E)	full of	colourful, beautiful
-fy, -ify (L)	make	satisfy, fortify
-hood (E)	state or condition of	boyhood, childhood
-ia (L)	names of classes, names of places	bacteria, America
-ian (L)	practioners or inhabitants	musician, Parisian
-ion (L)	condition or action of	persuasion
-ic (G)	relating to	historic
-id(e) (L)	a quality	acid
-ine (G; L)	a compound	chlorine
-ish (E)	a similarity or relationship	childish, greenish
-ism (G)	quality or doctrine of	realism, socialism
-itis (L)	inflammation of (medical)	bronchitis
-ist (G)	one who practices	chemist, pessimist
-ity, -ety, ty (L)	state or quality of	loyalty
-ive (L)	nature of	creative, receptive
-ize, -ise (G)	make, practise, act like	modernize, advertise
-less (E)	lacking	fearless, faceless
-logy (G)	indicating a branch of knowledge	biology, psychology
-lent (L)	fulness	violent
-ly (E)	having the quality of	softly, quickly
-ment (L)	act or condition of	resentment
-metry, -meter (G)	measurement	gasometer, geometry
-mony	resulting condition	testimony
-oid (G)	resembling	ovoid
-or (L)	a state or action, a person who, or thing which	error, governor, victor, generator
-ous, -ose (L)	full of	murderous, anxious, officious, morose
-osis	process or condition of	metamorphosis
-some	like	gladsome
-tude (L)	quality or degree of	altitude, gratitude
-ward (E)	direction	backward, outward
-y (E)	condition	difficulty

Vocabulary 2 (a)

1. .... is the condition of being marked with disgrace.
2. A .... is a woman who governs a nunnery.
3. Someone who has very strong nationalistic feelings and who makes a practice of this somewhat exaggerated patriotism is called a ....
4. That which is intractable, unruly, perverse; which goes in the wrong or unpredictable directions is ....
5. A .... is one who works in a certain field, such as medicine.
6. A .... is a comment or statement which has a high degree of insipidity and triteness.
7. The unpleasant medical condition in which part of the testicle becomes irritated and inflamed is known as ....
8. To .... is to imbue with the added qualities of courage, inspiration and fearlessness.
9. The doctrine of pursuing pleasure as the highest good is known as ....
10. If you are capable of working twelve hours a day without a rest; if you can engage in physical exercise for hours without seeming to get tired, then you are ....
11. Handwriting which is in the nature of a running hand; which forms the character rapidly without raising the pen is known as .... handwriting.
12. A .... is a small ornamental design, drawing or picture.
13. The quality or state of being uppermost, of having complete authority or power, is the state of ....
14. To .... is to render something unable to operate or move; to disband.
15. .... is the state of being bound or tied to something, either physically or mentally.

a. indefatigable   b. vignette   c. demobilize   d. epididymitis
e. practitioner   f. ignominy   g. supremacy   h. platitude
i. untoward   j. cursive   k. Chauvinist   l. prioress
m. hedonism   n. embolden   o. bondage

91

Vocabulary 2 (b)

1. Someone who places himself in a condition of suffering for his beliefs, is placing himself in a position of ....
2. A diminutive particle of matter is sometimes known as a ...., although this term now usually applies to the small particles constituting blood.
3. A girl who is joyful, attractive and engaging is ....
4. A charge for something which relates to the lowest or smallest price is ....
5. .... is the process in which fluids tend to mix, even through porous membranes.
6. A .... is a place where one goes to see models or projections of the solar system and other sections of the universe.
7. People who speak loudly and often are ....
8. .... is the state of being exhausted.
9. A rude girl or a tomboy is said to be ....
10. A .... person is full of antagonism and the desire to quarrel or fight.
11. A place where birds are kept is known as an ....
12. A .... look is one full of mischief or malice.
13. A .... is a person who holds high rank or status.
14. To be gentle, quiet, peaceful and serene is to be ....
15. An .... is that which provokes or produces discomfort or inflammation.

a. winsome b. minimal c. irritant d. enervation
e. vociferous f. bellicose g. aviary h. corpuscle
i. magnate j. hoydenish k. baleful l. placid m. osmosis
n. planetarium o. martyrdom

Vocabulary 2 (c)

1. To be filled with the desire to do nothing, to be lazy, phlegmatic and idle is to be ....
2. A .... is an eloquent speaker or writer.
3. The .... is that class of educated people who tend to form much of public opinion.
4. .... relates or pertains to the constant chemical changes in living matter.
5. An .... is any creature which resembles Man.
6. The branch of knowledge which deals with the body's organs and their functions is ....
7. A synonym for a state of boldness, courage and robustness is ....
8. That which is 'of the nature of the world' is often said to be ....
9. A disease the qualities of which are plague-like and virulent is often called a ....
10. .... is the act of having a contract or marriage abolished.
11. To look at one's self .... is to have the quality of the vain god who fell in love with his reflected image.
12. To .... is to raise to a higher or more extreme degree.
13. When we attribute to someone or something the quality of god-head we make him or it a ....
14. Someone whose appetites can not be satisfied is ....
15. The branch of knowledge which deals with the human mind and its functioning is ....

a. mundane   b. narcissistically   c. intelligentsia
d. insatiable   e. intensify   f. rhetorician   g. deity
h. psychology   i. physiology   j. pestilence   k. hardihood
l. annulment   m. anthropoid   n. metabolic   o. indolent

CHAPTER TWELVE

NOTE-TAKING

How often have you seen 'the diligent student' hanging on every word that his teacher or professor utters, and faithfully recording each gem in his notebook?! It is a fairly common sight, and one that brings a number of negative consequences.

First the person who is intent on getting everything down is like the reader who does not preview—he inevitably fails to see the woods (the general flow of argument) for the trees.

Second, a continuing involvement with getting things down prevents objective and on-going critical analysis and appreciation of the subject matter. All too often note-taking by-passes the mind altogether.

And third, the volume of notes taken in this manner tends to become so enormous, especially when combined with added notes from books, that when it comes to 'revising', the student finds he has to do almost the complete task again.

Proper note-taking is not a slavish following of what has been said or what has been written, but is a selective process which should minimise the volume of words taken down, and maximise the amount remembered from those words.

To achieve this we make use of the 'key-word' concept. A key-word is a word that encapsulates a multitude of meanings in as small a unit as possible. When that word is triggered, the meanings spray free. It can be effectively represented by the diagram on the next page.

Selecting key-words is not difficult. The first stage is to eliminate all the unnecessary surrounding language, so that if you came across the following statement in a science text: 'the speed of light has now been determined to be 186,000 miles per second' you would not write the whole sentence down but would summarise it as follows: 'light's speed = 186,000 m.p.s.'.

This is a crude example, but the principle behind it should

now be fairly clear to you. It is important to remember when making your notes with key-words that the key-words *must* trigger the right kind of remembering. In this respect words like 'beautiful', and 'horrifying', while being picturesque, are too general. They have many other meanings which might have nothing to do with the particular point you wish to remember.

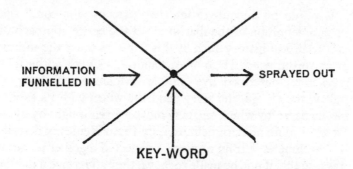

Further, a key-word should be one that you find personally satisfying and not one which you think somebody else might think is good. In many cases key-words need not be taken directly from the content of the lecture or the material being read. A word that you choose yourself and which summarises somebody else's words, is preferable.

If you practise key-word note-taking effectively you will be amazed at how much more information you can get into a given space.

As a matter of interest finish this day's reading by thumbing through some of your old notes from school or other sources, observing how much was completely unnecessary, and how much time you could have saved first in writing them down, and second in reading them back.

I think you will be surprised.

Your next Self-Test is on the History of the Machine. At this stage of your progress you should by now have consolidated your skimming and previewing techniques, and should have, in your daily practice, increased your reading speed by between 50 to 100 words per minute. In addition to this your critical and analytical abilities will now be considerably improved.

In this Self Test, preview (it should now be a habit!) and again push yourself to go just that little bit faster than Self Test 4.

After this reading practise your note-taking techniques on the material you have read. Your complete notes should not exceed half a page.

SELF TEST 5

THE HISTORY OF THE MACHINE

It would be difficult to find two persons who could agree upon a definition of the machine; yet the entire approach of a non-technical history such as this depends upon the meaning given to the word. Hero of Alexandria, a Greek authority on mechanics, described five 'simple' machines—the lever, the pulley, the wedge, the screw, and the wheel with its axle—as mechanisms 'by which one may move a given weight by a given force.' A more modern definition by Franz Reuleaux describes the machine as 'a train of pieces connected together in various ways, so that if one be made to move, they all receive a motion.' This seems to leave out Hero's machines altogether. Another definition is somewhat more inclusive—'an apparatus designed to transmit or multiply a force.' Note that this definition may be assumed to cover the tool—for it can be said that the force of human muscle is transmitted through the tool to increase human output.

Yet something still broader is needed, a definition which takes into account not only the machine itself but also the purpose of the machine in terms of human history, as well as the type of energy which activates it. Historically speaking, a machine might be described as a device (be it a simple lever, a gang of slaves, an ox and plow, or a steam engine) which helps man to get his work done, preferably increasing his output at the same time. One might add to this, machines such as the printing press, which have contributed to the diffusion of knowledge, and thus to the promotion of technical advance. Naturally, the form of energy put into the device is equally important in determining the historical importance of each class of machines. For thousands of years this was limited to human and animal muscle, and the power of wind and water.

In telling the story of Western civilization the history books generally dwell upon the great epochs of cultural and techno-logical advance, such as the flowering of Greece and the Italian

96

Renaissance. To these the archaeologists have added a period of profound and significant change—the break-through into civilization itself, about 3500 B.C. But of all the great epochs of Western civilization, the industrial revolution, in which we still find ourselves, may prove to be the most far-reaching of all. For it did not merely alter the attitudes and thinking of the privileged classes alone but changed the entire way of life, the manners, morals, customs, arts, and techniques of everybody, high or low, within its grasp. And it is still continuing to do so today in the so-called underdeveloped countries of the world.

At the center of the industrial revolution was the machine—the machine as prime mover, the machine in transportation, the machine turning out goods in factories or making the parts for still more machines. Not that there were no machines before the industrial revolution. But it is worth tracing, as we have here, the progress of the machine from ancient times to the Renaissance in order to see what a paucity of mechanical invention there was until the steam engine burst upon the world. As late as 1586 A.D., for example, people came from all over Europe to watch almost 1,000 men and 75 horses—pushing and tugging at a vast array of windlasses and levers—move an Egyptian obelisk some 900 feet to re-erect it in front of St. Peter's in Rome. Over 1,500 years earlier (no doubt using much the same methods) the Romans had brought this same obelisk all the way from Egypt.

Obviously the machine means little without its source of energy, and so we have chosen to emphasize not only the machine but its motive power—from human and animal muscle, through wind and water power, to steam, electricity, and the newer sources of energy available today. We have also touched here and there upon the social and economic effects of the machine.

In reviewing the history of the industrial revolution (which brought the machine into its own) it is surprising to find how far back it goes and yet how similar have been the problems and lines of progress from the beginning to the present. That typically American phenomenon, mass production for instance, began as early as 1798 when Eli Whitney of Connecticut, with a government order in his hand for 10,000 guns, worked out machine tools to produce the necessary parts on an interchangeable basis. A few years later Henry Maudslay, the great British engineer, set up 43 steam-driven machines at Portsmouth that turned out 10,000 wooden pulley blocks a year for the Royal Navy, replacing 110 craftsmen with ten unskilled men.

Early protests against the replacement of men by machines took the form of violence. Angry weavers forced John Kay, inventor in 1733 of the flying shuttle, to flee to France where he died in poverty. An automated grain mill at London, powered by one of Watt's early rotative engines, was destroyed by fire, probably set alight by irate older workmen, while in the 1840's in America Elias Howe's sewing machine was opposed by many who felt it would put thousands out of work. Today we are less violent, but we worry, and quite rightly, about the effects of automation—machines controlling machines, thus replacing men altogether.

And so the traditional themes continue: new sources of power appear, new technologies, new devices, and society continues to be progressively transformed by the continuing and ever-growing impact of the revolution. But there are differences. The initial industrial revolution was pioneered in England by self-made men in Birmingham and Lancaster, not by scholars in Oxford or Cambridge or London, and their approach to the new machines and factories was empirical: they improvised as they went along. George Stephenson, the great railway pioneer was a coalminer's son and had to teach himself to read and write. And as for the new processes: the chemistry of iron manufacture, for example, was not really understood until the end of the nineteenth century.

It was about this time, near the turn of the century, that the second industrial revolution can be said to have begun. Often called the scientific revolution, it represented a marriage between the industrial men, with their trial-and-error methods, and the theoreticians, the scholars and the scientists, who began to put their growing understanding of the basic operations of nature at the disposal of the industrialists. Empiricism gave way to theory, improvisation to calculated advances. It is this second phase of the industrial revolution in which we find ourselves today, and which is again transforming our entire world. And as always, the machine is at the heart of the greatest continuing revolution the world has ever known.

1. The entire approach to the history of the
machine depends upon the meaning given
to the word.   True   False

2. Five 'simple' machines were originally described by Plato.   True   False

3. A definition of the machine must take into
account the purpose of the machine in terms
of human history.   True   False

4. The form of energy put into a machine is
not significant in determining the historical
importance of each class of machine.   True   False

5. In telling the story of Western Civilisation
books do not dwell enough upon the great
epochs of cultural and technological ad-
vance.   True   False

6. The Industrial Revolution may prove to be
the most far reaching revolution of all.   True   False

7. Despite its great technological achievement,
the Industrial Revolution did not funda-
mentally affect morals or the arts.   True   False

8. The machine was the centre of the Industrial Revolution because before that time
there had been no machines.   True   False

9. The Egyptian obelisk was erected in 1566
A.D.   True   False

10. Mass production is a typically American
phenomena.   True   False

11. The replacement of men by machines was
originally seen as a tremendous social ad-
vance.   True   False

12. John Kay invented the early rotative engine. True   False

13. The Industrial Revolution in England was
brought about by self-made men.   True   False

14. The 'second Industrial Revolution' began
approximately 1600.   True   False

15. In the Scientific Revolution theory finally
gave way to empiricism.   True   False

CHAPTER THIRTEEN

THE BUZAN STUDY TECHNIQUE

We come now to the most important chapter of this book, for the method to be introduced here is applicable not only to certain academic materials, but may be applied to *anything* which is to be studied, ranging from the classical literature to the most complex higher mathematics and physics. The method is not directed toward a particular task, but provides the reader with a fundamental and all-inclusive approach to any material he wishes to study, with the confidence that he has the necessary background information at his fingertips.

I make bold to suggest that by contrast the popular and widely recommended SQ3R and PQRST methods, while generally adequate are not nearly so comprehensive and flexible as the method about to be described.

With the SQ3R method the reader first Surveys the material to be studied then asks himself Questions about what he wants to gain from the text, after which he Reads the material, Recites it, and finally Revises it. The PQRST method commences with a Preview followed by Question and a Reading after which the material is Summarised and finally Tested.

I hope it will be clear to the reader after he has considered the study method which is to be presented that neither of these approaches is adequate for the enormously varying demands made on the reader by study material.

Before describing my method, let me say a few words about the unfortunate aura that surrounds study books.

From the time that a child is introduced to text books at school until he has either completed his schooling or graduated from college, university or an institution of higher education, the text book is a continuing threat. Text books have proliferated out of all proportion, yet they *must* be studied, however reluctantly, for the dreaded examination questions are based on them. Many people develop a deep-rooted and almost mindless fear of any book that looks like a text book. Ask any university student when exam time is approaching!

If you have ever had occasion to observe some students study (especially if you're a mother or father.) you will have observed some such pattern as the following: Having decided to study on a certain evening the student will spend approximately five to ten minutes tidying and 'getting ready' his desk, making sure that everything is in exactly the right place before he starts. Just as he is about to sit down, however, he will 'remember' that there was an important telephone call he has to make and that if he doesn't make it he will be ill-at-ease during the study period. He makes the call (which is seldom brief!) and returns to his desk where he again adjusts the position of the study book, perhaps opens it and then suddenly 'remembers' that there is a television programme he was particularly interested in, so he goes to the next room in order to check the television schedules. Sure enough, it begins in fifteen minutes! As fifteen minutes is not enough time to commence studying he decides to wait until after the programme, rationalising that he will then be able to devote the next three hours of the evening to study, finishing off with another television programme which he happened to notice in the schedule.

The programme ends and our student (dare we call him that?) becomes aware of the fact that he is a little hungry and needs a snack of some sort which takes him ten minutes to prepare and twenty minutes to eat while he rereads the sports page for relaxation.

The snack, of course, makes him feel a bit drowsy, giving rise to the need for a short rest before the hard work of study, and this may as well be taken while watching the first ten minutes of another not very important but nevertheless fairly interesting programme on television.

The first ten minutes prove more interesting than anticipated, and after all, what is a brief extra twenty minutes when a whole two hours are to be devoted to diligent study afterwards!

Everyone knows, of course, that after a snack and an interesting television programme one should take a brief walk before getting down to work . . . and so it goes on and on until the evening has gone by, and anyway, tomorrow evening is always a far better time!

Do you recognise the situation? It reflects the point I made before about the underlying fear of books, and the consequent reluctance to grapple with them.

This fear may reach quite extraordinary proportions, and some of my own students, after having been tense for weeks on end, have come to me in a state of almost dreamlike happiness, explaining that they finally got rid of their haunting fear of study books by throwing all the texts they had against their study-room walls!

I am not recommending this as a solution for the syndrome is anything but humorous. Indeed, I mention it here to show how serious this problem actually is. The first step in overcoming it is to realise that text books are, actually, more easy to read than most other books, as long as one uses the right approach. Text books are usually laid out in clearly defined sections, each of which is linked in a rational way to the sections that precede and follow it.

The trouble is that most people tend not to use this information to the fullest advantage, and as a consequence get 'bogged down' in masses of detail.

Now, as I shall shortly advise you for all your reading, take a two minutes break before you start reading about my study method. It is divided into eight divisions, grouped into two parts of four each, the first entitled Preparation and the second Application.

THE BUZAN STUDY TECHNIQUE

A. Preparation

1. Setting the period of time to be devoted to each individual study session.

2. Deciding on the amount of material to be covered in the period of time allotted.

3. Reviewing present knowledge of the subject to be studied.

4. Setting down in question form what is to be gained from the material.

1. It is vitally important, before any study session, to decide reasonably closely how long that session is to be, and then to make certain that that time is indeed spent studying.

This is important because the mind learns best when it has a known boundary. The time limit sets such boundaries and also enables you to decide more accurately the amount of material to cover in the study session. Most people make the mistake of just sitting down to study for an undetermined time, only to find that they are wandering off into the distance, not knowing how far they will get nor how much material they will cover. What they end up with usually is a number of loose ends which contribute to both difficulty in understanding and rapidity in forgetting.

Having decided on the length of time to be devoted to study, say two hours, you should next divide the time into twenty-five minute sections with small breaks in between. This may sound a little disturbing, and the question might be asked 'but after half an hour I often feel really involved with what I am studying, won't the break destroy my understanding?'.

The answer lies in a distinction that must be made between what we understand and what we remember. These two concepts are often subconsciously confused, when in fact they are quite different. Think for example of all the books you have read. In many cases you will have understood them very well

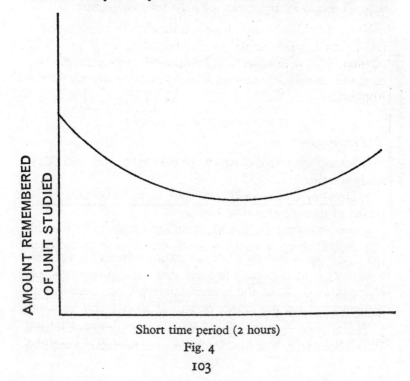

Short time period (2 hours)

Fig. 4

yet I am sure that now much of what you understood at the time and could still understand now has been totally forgotten.

Because these two concepts are confused most people think that when they are understanding well they will necessarily be remembering well. Nothing could be farther from the truth. Extensive research started at the end of the last century by Ebbinghaus, a German psychologist, and continued to the present day, has shown that regardless of the kind of material we are trying to remember, and regardless of our understanding, the retention curve for this material will be as shown in the preceding diagram.

It can be seen from this graph that *more* is remembered at the beginnings and ends of learning periods than is remembered in the middle. This 'middle sag' indicates that it is memory that has failed at this point, not understanding.

What we are concerned with in our apportioning of time is to make best use of the way in which memory works; and this we can do, as has been mentioned, by dividing study sections into smaller sections of approximately twenty-five minutes each. This may be represented by the following graph:

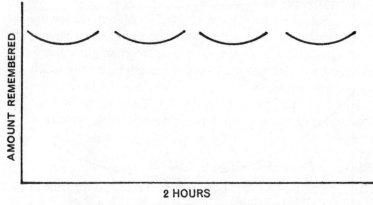

2 HOURS

Fig. 5

It will be seen that we now have eight relatively high points in memory instead of only two and that the memory sags are shallower for each of the shorter study periods than is the enormous sag for the longer period. It should also be clear from this graph, that, indirectly, understanding will be improved over the long run, because each new piece of informa-

tion reached will be considered in the light of more remembered knowledge. It will therefore be easier to understand.

I have taken a good deal of space to deal with this important
concept, but the decision itself should take no more than a
few seconds!

2. *Amount of Material to be Covered*

This second item in the study preparation section may come
first, if the material to be studied is a small and set piece. Usually however it will come second.

As I explained above, the mind functions far more happily
if it has well defined boundaries within which to work. Deciding on the amount of material to be covered does exactly this,
giving a *gestalt* or 'whole' in which the mind can work. If you
have ever sat through a lecture in which the speaker clearly outlined beforehand what he was going to cover, you will appreciate how much more satisfying it was and how much easier the
lecture was to understand. You were given a boundary, and
you knew the conclusion you were expected to reach. Deciding
on the amount of material you will cover in a study session does
the same thing.

In addition, these two 'boundary decisions' help reduce the
fear of study books discussed earlier. Once you know that you
have a certain amount of time in which to accomplish a self-
determined task, the task itself becomes much easier and much
more clearly defined. As a matter of fact, it is the uncertainty
factor (not knowing how much you are going to do, and not
knowing how long it is going to take) that reinforces the fear of
text books.

3. *Noting of Present Knowledge*

Having established the amount to be covered and the time in
which it is to be covered, we take the next step in gathering together what we already know about the subject. This is done
by having a quick mental run through our knowledge, noting
down general headings and ideas. The more that is known about
the subject the more general should be the headings. If little is
known, the notes should contain only the particular items of
knowledge.

It is most important that this run-through and jotting down

of notes be done as rapidly as possible—it should never take more than two minutes, and if you run out of time or information it is not important. What *is* important is that you go at full mental speed to gather the information, and that you note it in as a brief and concise a manner as possible.

Why do we do this? To establish what is known as 'mental set'. Mental set means that our brain is 'beamed in' properly to the kind of information that we trying to pick up. Noting down what we already know on the subject alerts the proper channels of the brain, enabling it to operate far more efficiently in the study context. If you have ever suffered from the problem of not being able to 'get in' to the material you have been reading you will see what I mean—for this problem is simply that the mind is still wandering in other channels.

This preparatory exercise might at first prove difficult, but you will find that it becomes easier and even enjoyable as you persevere. It is satisfying to know that you can readily call to mind information on a subject without hemming and hawing! To put it another way, this exercise will increase your ability to use what you know.

4. *Questions*

The fourth and last section of study preparation is to ask yourself initial questions about what you want to get from the material you will be reading: in other words, define your aims.

These questions, like the items of knowledge, should be quickly jotted down and should never take more than two minutes. They, like the knowledge section, help establish a mental set and also act as hooks for gathering in information as you go through the book. This is because understanding and memory rely heavily on what are known as associative processes, which simply means that things are better understood and memorised when they are linked or hooked together.

In some cases you will be starting to read a new book about which you know very little and about which it will be difficult to ask questions. In such cases the little formula of 'how?', 'when?', 'where?', 'why?', 'what?' and 'who?' or 'by whom?' should serve quite adequately.

You will have noted that I said 'initial' questions. This is because further questions can be asked after one has completed the first two steps of the Application section, the Survey and Preview. It should be noted that, as in the knowledge section, the time set aside for asking questions should be *very brief*.

B. *Application*

Having defined our boundaries, gathered our present knowledge together, and set out our hooks for gathering new knowledge we are now ready to apply ourselves with greater confidence to the material. As with the Preparation section the Application part is divided into four basic divisions.

1. Survey.
2. Preview.
3. Inview.
4. Review.

1. *Survey*

In the survey we start by looking at the outer and inner covers of the book in order to gather whatever significant information we can. After this look quickly at the introductory pages and then read fairly carefully through the table of contents. This as I mentioned in the Preface gives one a general overview of what is to be covered. Following this go through the whole book or the section of the book that is to be covered looking at everything which is not part of the regular print. This means that the following will be included in your survey: chapter headings, photographs, diagrams, illustrations, subheadings, marginal comments, footnotes, italics, emphasised words, tables, lists, and indexes.

The purpose of the survey can be likened to the framework of a house that is being built—it gives us a basic structure onto which we can build the particular details and embellishments.

In cases of books which contain a large number of statistical tables, the mathematically oriented reader can take comfort in the knowledge that if he quickly understands the graphs he will probably not have to read so much or so deeply for many of the words in the book will probably be explaining the graphs that he has already understood. On the other side of this coin the reader who prefers a language explanation to a graphic explanation can rest reasonably assured that the graph that he does not understand will be explained for him in the body of the text. A survey is usually quite brief.

2. *Preview*

Having established the basic structure we now go through the remainder of the material, that is, the main body of print. We are not ready as yet to read this material for complete understanding as we want to fill in a little more of the basic structure before doing this. In the preview we skim over material not covered in the survey, looking for main pointers on the direction the explanations are taking. At this stage in your reading progress it is best to concentrate on initial and final paragraphs of chapters or sections and on proper nouns. These you will find almost loom out of the print at you. In the preview special attention should be paid to any summary, conclusion or results section, for you will often find that these sections contain as much as 90% of the information you require.

In the preview, as in the survey, it is most important that you develop your powers of selection and rejection. So much time is wasted by readers who get to the end of a whole section only to realise near the end that they need not have read any of it! Obviously one does not wish to reject at random, but such things as an author's repetition of a point you already fully understand, long lists of examples which are not relevant to your purpose, and even entire sections which deal with aspects of the subject that you already know about or which are of no importance to your purpose in studying, should be watched for.

3. *Inview*

Our survey and preview now completed, and our basic idea of the structure of the material we are studying now well established, we are ready, if we still find it necessary, to progress to the inview. In this section we read carefully through the material filling in the areas that were left out in the survey and preview. Even at this stage, however we must be prepared to leave very important or very difficult sections to a later stage, as mulling over them for too long breaks the train of thought and, while perhaps giving us a little better understanding of that section, diminishes our understanding of the whole.

I shall once again break with tradition here and recommend that at these difficult or important points in the text a very soft pencil be used to make a faint line *in the margin* (not underneath the lines) next to the appropriate text.

4. Review

This is the final stage of study reading, in which we integrate all the material into a meaningful whole. It is during the review that I recommend the taking of notes, for it is only at this point in the study process that we can be fully aware of the importance of the general themes and of the details. There is no need to worry about forgetting what was considered to be important, for the pencil marks in the margin should serve as adequate reminders. Even so some people do find it a little difficult to 'hold themselves back' in the taking of notes, and in such cases notes can be made during the survey, preview, and main reading, although they should be as brief as possible.

The study technique as outlined above might seem at first glance to be a straightforward and even rigid approach but it is in fact very flexible, and can be modified to fit appropriate material.

In most situations the first four stages are indispensable because they are simply a preparation for study, regardless of the subject to be studied. It does not matter whether we are studying physics or literature, we still need goals and a positive direction.

When we come to the four stages of application, however, the picture changes. In many cases, especially in the study of mathematics and physics, it is advisable to survey the material more than once. In the case of one student I taught at Oxford University we found that the only way for him to cover his higher mathematics successfully was for him to survey the material *twenty times* with the result that a chapter which had baffled him for 4 months was 'solved' in 3 weeks!

In literary material there is often virtually nothing to survey, in which case this step may be skipped and if it is felt necessary, an extra preview may be added.

Still other situations can arise. It may turn out for instance that after a survey, or preview, or both, further reading is not necessary. In such a case there is certainly no point in continuing other than to take notes, should they be desired. Yet again the reader may feel that his final review was not quite sufficient and wish to re-review so to speak.

The Application section of this technique, in other words, gives you the basic tools with which to operate, and it is up to you to use them in as intelligent and as appropriate a manner as the situation demands. Unlike other study techniques, you are *not* restricted to an unbreakable pattern—you are given an approach that is universally applicable and at the same time individually adjustable.

The next Self Test selection is on slightly more diffiuclt material, and as a result you may find a slight decrease in your performance scores. Do not be concerned about this, as most people, when reading material of this difficulty, seldom complete it at an average of more than 90 w.p.m. If you can score near your previous progress scores you are a phenomenon!

Your approach to this Self Test should be as follows: first apply all the techniques you have learnt previous to this chapter, and second, use the Study Technique in the reading. Quickly Survey the material, looking at headings and underlined words, Preview as suggested, and then Inview and Review as necessary. For the purpose of this exercise you need take no notes.

SELF TEST 6

HISTORY

I. *The Prehistoric Period*

I. *Definition, Data, and Methods*

History in its broadest sense should be a record of Man and his accomplishments from the time when he ceased being merely an animal and became a human being. The efforts to reconstruct this record may be classed under two heads:

(1) <u>History</u> (in the stricter sense), which is based on written documents and covers part of the last five thousand years of Man's activities, and

(2) <u>Prehistory</u> which is based largely on archaeological evidence and covers all the long preceding period, which probably amounts to more than one million years.

The prehistoric period is important, not only by reason of its vast length, but also because during this time Man made almost all his major discoveries and adaptations to environment and group-life (except those connected with the recent machine age) and evolved physically into the modern racial types. Hence at least a brief summary of the prehistoric period is a necessary introduction to any account of the recorded history of Man.

The main body of material upon which the work of prehistoric reconstruction is based comprises: <u>first</u>, remains left by early peoples, largely in the form of tools and other artifacts, found by excavation in old habitation sites or burials; <u>secondly</u> other traces of their activities, such as buildings and rock-carvings or rock-paintings; and <u>lastly</u>, the bones of the people themselves. This material gives good evidence of their language. It can be supplemented to some extent—and with great caution—by a comparative study of the physical types, languages, and material culture of modern peoples.

The time when prehistory ends and true history begins varies greatly in different parts of the world. Traditional history often covers the borderline between the two and can sometimes be successfully correlated with the archaeological evidence.

In prehistory, dates are entirely a matter of estimate and cannot be used as fundamental landmarks, as in the case of recorded history.

2. The Origin of Man

<u>Man's place among the Animals</u>. The various living and extinct species of Man are assigned by zoologists to the family Hominidae, which belongs to the sub-order <u>Anthropoidea</u> (containing monkeys, apes and baboons), of the order <u>Primates</u> (containing also Tarsius and the lemurs) of the class Mammalia. His nearest living relatives are the four genera of the family <u>Simiidae</u> (the so-called Anthropoid Apes): the gorilla and chimpanzee of equatorial Africa and the orang-utan and gibbon of southeastern Asia and the East Indies. Man is distinguished from the higher apes by the greater size of his

brain (especially the forebrain), his fully erect position in walking, the better adaption of his hands for grasping and holding, and his use of language for communication.

Man's Animal Ancestors. No remains have yet been found of Man's immediate precursor, the primitive and more ape-like animal from which he is supposed to be descended. Neither have we yet found any certain traces of the postulated animal (often popularly termed the Missing Link) from which both Man and the anthropoid apes are descended. Several forms of fossil apes have been found, however, which show a kinship to Man in some particulars and help to bridge over this gap: notably, Propliopithecus, from the Lower Oligocene of Egypt; Sivapithecus, from Miocene India; Dryopithecus, from Miocene France; and Australopithecus (the 'Taungs skull') from the Pliocene or Pleistocene of South Africa.

Date of Man's Origin. This has not yet been definitely established. The ancestors of the great apes and the ancestor of Man probably diverged from one another as early as the Miocene period, and Man acquired certain essentially human characteristics probably in the Pliocene period. The earliest known skeletal remains that are accepted as human are believed to date from the early or middle part of the Pleistocene period. For the purposes of the prehistorian, who has to rely largely on archaeological evidence, the record of Man may be said to begin at the moment when he was able to fashion the first stone tools which can be unmistakably recognised to be of human workmanship. This was early in the Pleistocene, or possibly in the very late Pliocene.

Place of Man's Origin. This is still entirely a matter of speculation. The old theory of Central Asia as the 'Cradle of Mankind' was based on false premises, which have been abandoned. From the distribution of the living and fossil great apes, it is thought that Man's divergence from the general anthropoid stem is likely to have taken place somewhere in the area comprising western Europe, the northern half of Africa, and southern Asia, with the preference perhaps slightly in favour of Africa or Asia, but there is no real evidence at present to warrant a final conclusion.

3. Cultures and Their Dating

a. Cultures and Period

Archaeological investigation of the material remains of prehistoric Man has shown that a wide variety of cultures flourished in different parts of the world and at different times. For convenience these have been grouped into a series of major cultures based primarily on the nature of the principal material used for implements (whether stone or one of the metals), and sometimes on the technique used in fashioning these implements. The oldest culture in the world was characterised by the use of chipped stone for implements and has been named Palaeolithic culture. Neolithic culture, on the other hand, was characterized by the use of polished stone implements; Bronze culture, by the use of bronze implements and so forth.

In most parts of the world the discovery and use of these different materials and techniques took place in a regular sequence in time. In the absence of fixed dates, it was thus found convenient to use these cultural terms in a chronological sense. Accordingly prehistoric times have usually been divided into the following series of periods of ages (beginning with the oldest):

Palaeolithic (old stone) characterised by chipped stone implements;

Mesolithic (Intermediate stone) a transitional period;

Neolithic (new stone) with polished stone implements:

Chalcolithic (Stone and copper) characterised by the first tentative use of copper implements;

Bronze Age with full development of copper and bronze implements; and

Iron Age with iron implements.

These names are excellent to identify cultures, but their use to designate periods of time has led to much inaccuracy and confusion, as the dates of the cultures to which they refer differ widely in different parts of the world. It is proper, for example, to speak of the Bronze Age of Hungary or some other limited area, where the beginning and end of the bronze culture can be fairly accurately dated. But it is quite impossible to speak with any meaning of the Bronze Age of the Old World for this period began some thousand or fifteen hundred years earlier in Mesopotamia, for instance, than it did in western Europe, and it gave way to the Iron Age one or two thousand years earlier in Asia Minor than it is in some parts of Siberia; while in Japan there was no true Bronze Age and in Australia no Bronze Age at all. The names of these periods are, however, too well established to be abandoned and are often useful, if employed with caution.

TEST 6 (1,210 words)

1. History in its broadest sense should be a record of the evolution of life.	True False
2. Pre-history is based largely on archaeological evidence.	True False
3. Pre-history is important because man made most of his discoveries and adaptation during this period.	True False
4. Tools and artifacts found by excavation form a large part of our collection of the remains left by early peoples.	True False
5. The division between pre-history and history is fairly constant geographically and chronologically.	True False
6. Living and extinct species of man are assigned to the family Tarsius.	True False
7. Man's nearest living relatives are the four genera of the family Simidiae	True False
8. Man's immediate predecessor remains a mystery.	True False
9. The date of Man's origin has been established within a period of a thousand years.	True False
10. The record of Man may be said to begin at the moment when he was able to fashion the first stone tool.	True False
11. The 'Cradle of Mankind' places Man's origin in central Asia.	True False
12. There is no real evidence to warrant a final conclusion on the place of Man's origin.	True False

13. Early cultures are identified by the growth of language and communication.   True   False
14. The names of Ages such as Bronze and Iron have led to inaccuracy and confusion.   True   False
15. The names of the periods of the development of Man should be abandoned.   True   False

N.B.—The remembering of material learnt while applying the study technique can be made much easier by using memory systems. I have covered this extensively in my book *Speed Memory* (published by Sphere Books) donating a special section to examinations.

CHAPTER FOURTEEN

LITERATURE AND POETRY

It is obviously not possible to give a comprehensive dissertation on the novel in this book but I hope that the points to be discussed in this chapter will encourage you to take a wider interest in this form of writing, and subsequently to read more widely about the approaches to its appreciation.

To make the discussion more comprehensible I shall discuss separately the following aspects of the novel as an art: plot, theme, philosophy, stand-point, character development, mood and atmosphere, setting, imagery, symbolism, and language.

Plot

Plot is the basic structure of events in the novel; the story-line, if you wish. It may range from a relatively minor role in primarily descriptive writing to a major role in the better *Who-Done-Its* and mystery novels.

Theme

The theme is what the plot is about. For example in *The Forsyte Saga*, a series of novels which deal with the history of a Victorian family, the theme might variously be considered to be capitalism versus creativity, conservatism versus liberalism, conformity versus individuality or riches versus poverty. Sub-themes which run parallel to the main one often occur in novels. Sub-themes often concern minor love affairs and secondary characters.

Philosophy

Philosophy is the system of ideas governing the universe of the work, and can often be thought of as the author's comment on the themes with which the book deals. Novelists known for the philosophical content in their novels include Dostoevesky, Sartre and Thomas Mann.

Stand-Point

This is *not* necessarily the author's point of view or personal feeling about what he is writing but the physical stand-point from which the events described are seen. The author may, for instance, be all-knowing, standing apart and viewing past, present and future of the event he is describing (Henry James advocated abandoning this device as he felt it clouded true representation).

In opposition to this omniscient point of view, the author may place himself in the first person (the author becomes the 'I' of the book) as in Hammond Innes' adventure stories and *Lolita* by Nabokov.

Character Development

Character development concerns the changes the persons in the story undergo. It may range from one extreme like Fleming's James Bond, who remains completely unchanged throughout his series, to Etienne in Zola's *Germinal* who develops from a rebellious youth into a mature and dedicated man.

Mood and Atmosphere

These two terms refer to the manner in which the author evokes reality or unreality and the emotional response of the reader. Some people prefer to use only one of these terms, although they can be distinguished when placed together: mood can be described as the reaction felt by the individual to the atmosphere of a piece of writing. For example, the atmosphere in Poe's stories might be described as morbid and menacing, while the mood of his readers might vary from depressed to exhilarated.

Setting

Setting refers to the physical locale and the time period in which the events take place. Because the setting is usually quite apparent, its importance is often underestimated—yet the slightest variations in time and place are often very significant. Recently the setting has become even more important because of its close links with symbolism.

Imagery

Imagery is often described as the use of simile and metaphor in language, meaning that items and events are described in creative or fanciful language. The root word 'image' is perhaps most useful in coming to an understanding of this term. Examples: Sir Walter Scott, in *The Heart of Midlothian*, described Edinburgh as 'the pulsating heart core of the Scottish scene'; and Dickens, in his *Tale of Two Cities* when describing the uncovering of a prisoner buried alive for eighteen years uses images of death and burial—heavy wreaths, cadaverous colours and emaciated heads and figures. Darkness and shadows prevail.

Symbolism

Simply explained, symbolism means that one thing stands for or represents another. Throughout much of literary history the Earth for example has symbolised fertility and reproduction.

Since the theories of Freud, symbolism has become an increasingly important factor in literature with a new emphasis on the sexual. Any jutting object such as a gun or tree is used to symbolise the male sex organs, and any circular or hollow object such as a box or a pond is used to symbolise the female sex organs. An excellent example of symbolism can be found in *The Tale of Two Cities*, when a cask of red wine is spilt. The populace drink the muddy dregs with relish, signifying the hungry despair which later results in the spilling of real blood in the French Revolution. In D. H. Lawrence's *The Fox* the frozen waste in which two women live symbolises their frigidity which is attacked by the male character who eliminates a fox (symbolising the general male 'threat'). His killing of the fox with his gun places him in the dominant male role.

Symbolism may be much more obscure than in these examples, and the reader who misses it often also misses the main point of the story.

Language

Authors' use of language varies from the tough masculine style of Hemingway to the flowing and poetic language of

Nabokov. The language an author uses is always revealing, and if the reader pays careful attention to it he will often gain far deeper insight into the shades of meaning and mood within the work.

In discussing aspects of style in the novel I have dealt with each item separately, but should like to make clear that each is inseparably linked to all the others. The very setting of a story, for example, may be symbolic—and so it is with the other aspects. When you read literature, always try to be aware of the intricate interlacings and interrelationships of the aspects that have been discussed.

Poetry

Many people insist that poetry should be read very slowly. Our talking speed is about 200 words a minute, but many of us tend to read poetry at less than 100. Actually this hinders a proper appreciation, for a slow, plodding trudge through a poem effectively destroys the natural rhythm, and in consequence conceals much of the meaning from the reader. In schools this problem is made worse by teachers who fail to correct students when they read each line as though the meaning lay at the end. This is often simply *not* true. Sophisticated poets let their meaning flow through all the lines.

The best approach to the reading of poetry is as follows:

1. A very rapid preview, enabling the reader to find out roughly what the poem is about and where it leads.

2. A second rapid but more thorough reading to get a more accurate idea of the way in which the lines relate to each other and the way in which the thought and rhythm interlink and progress.

3. A leisurely ramble through the poem concentrating on areas of particular interest.

4. A reading aloud.

In the final analysis speed is often irrelevant in an approach to literature and poetry—the situation becoming more like listening to music or appreciating art. One does not listen to Beethoven's 5th Symphony once and disregard it with the triumphant claim 'Well, I've done that at an average speed of 33 r.p.m.!'

When reading literature and poetry, bring to bear all your

knowledge and judgment, and if you feel that it is the kind of writing you wish to treasure forever, forget about *speeding through it* and reserve it for those occasions when time is not so pressing.

Self Test 7 is the first of two essays dealing with the History of Art. From now on there is no need for you to apply the full study technique in the Self Tests. Your approach should be to apply *whatever* seems most appropriate from all that you have learned. In other words, you should now begin to make your own decisions about the way in which you will tackle any given material.

As you have done in the previous Self Tests, continue with your endeavour to improve on previous performances.

SELF TEST 7

PERIODS, SCHOOLS AND STYLES

Art—Primitive to Christian

Primitive Art

It is essential for the observer to have at least an outline background of the historical development of pictorial art, and to take first a brief glance at its prehistoric and primitive forms. All the arts have their origin in prehistoric times, but the representations of animals incised on ivory and bone or drawn and painted on the walls and ceilings of caves in the north of Spain and south of France still excite wonder by their exceptional power and 'modernity'. Masterpieces were produced between (to give very rough limits) 40,000 B.C. and 10,000 B.C. What we notice in the photographs or outline copies made from them is the way in which the artist has selected and emphasized the main characteristics of the animals—mammoth and bison, deer, wild boar and wild horse—depicted; the knowledge he displays of their anatomy; the solid bulk and vigorous movements he conveys with no more than a little black and red ochre.

The period during which they were produced is longer than all recorded history, but there are comparable paintings and drawings by people living a similar life at a much later date. Thus the African bushman has left, in rock-shelters, drawings of animals as beautiful as those of our first European artists and resembling them in style, though some are as recent as the 19th century of our era. The realism of these hunting folk is not repeated in the art of the next stage of civilization, when social life takes a more definite form, when tools of stone and bronze are perfected, the crafts of pottery and weaving are pursued and, with the growth of agriculture, various rites and ceremonies propitiating the elements come into being. The typical primitive society, of which there still remain various survivals as in Polynesia, is largely concerned in the arts with its rudimentary religion. Carving and sculpture exceed painting in importance: the idol in three dimensions more impressively represents the powers assumed to affect primitive life. Painting and drawing are reduced to a series of signs and symbols. This, in a way seems a step backwards from the art of the cave-man though it must be remembered that the latter was less well organized. The cave-man could draw a single animal superbly: he had not yet learnt to set a group in ordered relation—often one image is superimposed on another in the most heedless way. It is with the later primitive society that the idea of painting as decoration comes into being.

The Ancient Mediterranean World

Painting and drawing in the ancient Mediterranean world has three aspects. There is first the wall painting, with bold outline and flat colour, the technique somewhat resembling that of certain modern posters. The ancient Egyptians used it on the exteriors of their temples: a sharply defined low relief providing an outline which was filled with bright colour. The majority of surviving Egyptian paintings are those of tomb walls, including scenes from the life of the deceased. A number of conventional devices are regularly used, for example, the male figure is painted in red ochre, the female, in yellow; the head and legs are always in profile however otherwise the body is turned. A great quality, however, is the lively observation which appears in scenes of banqueting and dancing or fishing and fowling along the Nile. The wall paintings of ancient Crete discovered in the palace of Knossos afford a parallel with those of Egypt in their bright, flat colours and decided outlines, though entirely secular in character.

The painted pottery of ancient Greece offers on a small scale something of these traditional styles. The male figure is dark, the female figure light, and outline plays a dominant part. The Greek vase painters (who often signed their cups and vases) can be studied as draughtsmen with a most exquisite sense of value of line and silhouette. In the classical period, however, the art of vase painting ceased to occupy an important place, and it is now that we first come upon the record of pictures in the modern sense, though our idea of them is unfortunately not based on the authentic works of the legendary masters, Zeuxis or Apelles, but on copies of Greek painting discovered when the Roman cities Pompeii and Herculaneum were excavated. It is clear enough however, that the Greek painters had given the art a scope and character undreamed of by the Egyptians or Minoans. Their work was no longer flat, but represented light and shade. The Greeks conceived dramatic figure compositions; they interested themselves in the problem of giving individual character and expression to their figures, in features and gesture. The Greco-Roman works that adorned the villas of wealthy Romans in the 1st century A.D. provide examples of landscape (previously unknown) and of still-life studied for its own sake. They forecast the later development of painting in Italy.

Byzantine Art

The dissolution of the Roman Empire, the establishment of a new Rome in the former Byzantium (Constantinople), and the emergence of Christianity as the universal creed of the West gave to painting a new character, spirit and aim. The Christian religion was now the artist's theme. A formal style now known as Byzantine, suited to express its earnestness and ritual, grew up. Constantinople had many links with the East, whose influence is to be seen in the use of rich colour.

The main triumphs of Byzantine pictorial art were achieved in mosaic, on the walls or the curved surface of the inner domes of the Byzantine church. Its other forms were, firstly, the icon, the image of Christ or the Virgin, represented, of set purpose, in a fixed convention which in itself declared the unalterable nature of belief; and secondly the illumination of manuscript Gospels and liturgical works with painting and gold. The style of these is as unchanging as that of the icon. The Byzantine capital remained intact, prosperous and fixed in its ways for 1,100 years after its foundation in the 4th century A.D., so that works very similar in many respects, may vary considerably in date. The sphere of Byzantine art corresponds to the sphere of influence of the Byzantine Empire: the eastern shores of the Mediterranean, Greece and the Greek islands. To some extent it was carried westward, with the movements of Byzantine missionaries and craftsmen. The famous 8th-century Irish manuscript, the Book of Kells, has its links of style with the eastern Mediterranean. The Italian cities Florence, Siena and Pisa had a Byzantine tradition, the end of which is marked by the painting of Cimabue in Florence and Duccio in Siena in the 13th century. In eastern Europe what is now Yugoslavia has remarkable Byzantine wall paintings of the 12th to 14th centuries. Greek painters introduced the icon into Russia and the Russian Andrew Roublev (c. 1360–c. 1430) brought the style to a magnificent pitch of development. Crete remained a centre until the 16th century and there is still a trace of the Byzantine tradition in the paintings of El Greco (c. 1545–1614).

Early Christian Art in the West

East or west, early Christian art in general avoided the realistic imitation of the human form that had been a feature of classical art. Yet it was not necessarily crude and imperfect, but more spiritual and abstract, in the sense of being removed from mundane affairs; and from this point of view it is nowadays judged more favourably than it used to be. Early Christian art in the west has an intricate history. It followed first the Greco-Roman tradition as in the paintings of the Roman catacombs. It was modified by the local character of the various regions into which the Roman Empire was re-grouped. It was affected by its communications, religious and commercial, with the Eastern Empire. The monastic art of the illuminated manuscripts was for a long time the main form of pictorial art, as in Celtic and Anglo-Saxon Britain and in the empire of Charlemagne. Two things became increasingly clear with time: that Christianity was the one unifying and educational force in

Europe, and that pictures were a principal means of conveying its message effectively and universally among people speaking different tongues or unable to read and write. With the great period of church building, from the 11th century, the international western style known as Romanesque developed. Its greatest products were the wall paintings of churches. Working on a large area, the painters developed a bold and simple style of much grandeur.

1. All the arts have their origin in pre-historic times.   True   False

2. 'Masterpieces' were produced even by primitive men.   True   False

3. The African Bushman, unlike the Caveman, did not concern himself so much with animals.   True   False

4. The typical primitive society is largely concerned in the arts with religion.   True   False

5. Early religion made art more symbolic.   True   False

6. Ancient Mediterranean wall painting is distinguished by fine outlines and brilliant colours.   True   False

7. Egyptian paintings made use of a number of conventional devices.   True   False

8. In the classical period of Greek painting the vase began to occupy an important place.   True   False

9. Much of our knowledge of this period is based on the work of the Greek masters Zeuxis and Apelles.   True   False

10. The Greeks were not particularly concerned with the representation of light and shade.   True   False

11. Byzantine art made Christianity the artists' theme.   True   False

12. The links of Constantinople with the east can be seen in Byzantine art in the rich colour.   True   False

13. The Byzantine school lasted approximately 500 years.   True   False

14. Early Christian art in the west attempted to imitate the human form realistically.   True   False

15. The Romanesque style developed in conjunction with an increase in Church building.   True   False

CHAPTER FIFTEEN

VOCABULARY (3)

This is the last of the vocabulary chapters and it deals with word roots (words from which others are derived).

As in the earlier chapters dealing with vocabulary, a list is given, this time of word roots, their translated meanings, and an example of a word containing the root. This is followed by the kind of vocabulary test with which you have now become familiar.

As this is the last chapter dealing with words and their meanings, I should like to offer a few hints on how you may continue to improve your vocabulary:

First, perform the exercise mentioned in Chapter 11; that is, browse through a good dictionary, studying the various ways in which the prefixes, suffixes and roots you have learnt are used. Keep a record of noteworthy examples and useful words.

Second, make a continuing and concentrated effort to introduce into your vocabulary at least one new word a day. New words are retained only if they are repeated a number of times, so once you have selected your word or words make sure that you use them often and effectively.

Third, be on the look-out for new and exciting words in conversations. If you are embarrassed about asking a speaker to define his terminology, make a quick mental note or jot the word down and look it up later.

Fourth, keep an eagle-eye out for unfamiliar words in anything you read. *Don't* write them down as you read, but make a mark with a pencil as indicated in Chapter 13 and look them up afterwards.

And *finally* if you feel so inclined, go to your library or local bookshop and ask for a book on vocabulary training—there are a number and most of them are quite helpful.

ROOTS
LATIN AND GREEK

Root	Meaning	Example
aer	air	aerate, aeroplane
am (fr. amare)	love	amorous, amateur, amiable

Root	Meaning	Example
ann (fr. annus)	year	annual, anniversary
aud, (fr. audire)	hear	auditorium, audit
bio	life	biography
cap (fr. capire)	take	captive
cap (fr. caput)	head	capital, per capita, decapitate
chron	time	chronology, chronic
cor	heart	cordial
corp	body	corporation
de	god	deify, deity
dic, dict	say, speak	dictate
duc, (fr. ducere)	lead	aqueduct, duke, ductile
ego	I	egotism
equi	equal	equidistant
fac, fic, (fr. facere)	make, do	manufacture, efficient
frat	brother	fraternity
geo	earth	geology
graph	write	calligraphy, graphology, telegraph
loc (fr. locus)	place	location, local
loqu, loc (fr. loqui)	speak	eloquence, circumlocution
luc, (fr. lux)	light	elucidate
man (fr. manus)	hand	manuscript, manipulate
mit, miss (fr. mittere)	send	admit, permission
mort, (fr. mors)	death	immortal
omni	all	omnipotent, omnibus
pat (fr. pater)	father	paternal
path	suffering, feeling	sympathy, pathology
ped, (fr. pes)	foot	impede, millepede, pedal
photo	light	photography
phobia, phobe	fear	hydrophobe, xenophobia
pneum	air, breath, spirit	pneumonia
pos, posit	place	deposit, position
pot, poss, poten, (fr. ponerte)	be able	potential, possible
quaerere	ask, question, seek	inquiry, query
rog, (fr. rogare)	ask	interrogate
scrib, scrip, (fr. scribere)	write	scribble, script, inscribe
sent, sens, (fr. sentire)	feel	sensitive, sentient
sol	alone	soloist, isolate
soph	wise	philosopher
spect, (fr. spicere)	look	introspective, inspect
spir, (fr. spirate)	breathe	inspiration
therm, (fr. thermos)	warm	thermometer
ten, (fr. tendere)	stretch	extend, tense
ten, (fr. tenere)	hold	tenant
utilis	useful	utility
ven, vent (fr. venire)	come, arrive	advent, convenient
vert, vers, (fr. vertere)	turn	revert, adverse
vid, vis (fr. videre)	see	supervisor, vision, provident

Vocabulary 3 (a)

1. A person who is friendly and lovable is often described as ....

2. A .... is a wise or would-be learned man.

3. Material through which light can travel is ....

4. You are .... if you are unable to perform or act.

5. An .... is a payment made yearly.

6. When an actor stands alone on the stage and speaks to himself his speech is known as a ....

7. The word ...., which now usually means to pass away or die, derives from the idea of breathing out.

8. If a bone is out of joint, or misplaced, we say it is ....

9. The transference of thoughts from one mind to another over a distance is known as ....

10. .... means to be alike in proportion, value or structure; to be in a corresponding position.

11. A person who is quarrelsome and discontented, and who complains in a questioning manner, is ....

12. .... means pertaining to heat.

13. A trial hearing of an applicant for employment, especially in the case of actors and singers, is known as an ....

14. .... is the controversial art of analysing personality from handwriting.

15. If you suffer from a fear of open spaces, you suffer from ....

a. expire   b. translucent   c. audition   d. sophist
e. annuity   f. agoraphobia   g. querulous   h. amiable
i. thermal   j. dislocated   k. graphology   l. impotent
m. telepathy   n. soliloquoy   o. homologous

Vocabulary 3 (b)

1. If you behead someone you .... him.
2. A .... person is one who will stretch a point in order to convince.
3. .... is the study of the physical features of the crust of the earth.
4. To .... is to take complete control of the attention; to overcome by charm of manner and appearance.
5. A person who considers himself to be the centre of the universe is described as ....
6. ...., a term usually reserved for God, is occasionally applied to people who seem to know everything.
7. A .... is someone who holds that actions are right only if they are useful.
8. An .... is a statement which comes between a person and his intended action; a prohibition.
9. The murder of one's own father is known as ....
10. If something is made by, or results from art; if it is in some way artificial, we say it is ....
11. The .... is that time of year when both day and night are of equal length.
12. A .... is a steward or servant (someone who waits on you hand and foot!).
13. .... means to cause to come together; to call to an assembly.
14. That which has a material body is said to be ....
15. .... is leading or carrying away, usually by fraud or force.

a. tendentious   b. fractitious   c. convene   d. decapitate
e. corporeal   f. manciple   g. equinox   h. captivate
i. abduction   j. egocentric   k. geomorphology   l. omniscient
m. interdict   n. utilitarian   o. patricide

Vocabulary 3 (c)

1. A person who is destitute of sense or given to extremes, we call ....
2. .... is the power of projecting one's feelings into an object or person, and so reach full understanding.
3. ....means to shed light on, to make clear.
4. A .... drill is one that uses compressed air.
5. An instrument that finely measures time is a ....
6. A .... person is one who holds on, no matter what the circumstances.
7. A .... is money sent to you.
8. The science which deals with the forces exerted by air and by gaseous fluids is ....
9. The germinal matter for all living things is ....
10. When people associate as brothers, we say they ....
11. If something is .... it reminds us of death.
12. An .... may be defined as the act of placing or putting on; a burden, often unwelcome.
13. .... is when you substitute someone else for yourself in regard to asking for your legal rights.
14. .... refers to that which is deserted, laid waste, solitary, forsaken.
15. .... is a feeling of giddiness.

a. chronometer   b. imposition   c. subrogation   d. elucidate
e. insensate   f. desolation   g. morbid   h. vertigo
i. remittance   j. fraternise   k. empathy   l. pneumatic
m. bioplasm   n. aerodynamics   o. tenacious

The next Self Test is the second of the two essays on the History of Art. As you are already familiar with the basic style and approach of this author, you should be able to make an accurate assessment of the difficulty of the material, and should be able to decide fairly easily on the best approach to this material. See if you can improve your speed performance on this reading by 50 words per minute!

SELF TEST 8

GOTHIC—THE NATIONAL SCHOOLS

Gothic Art

The monumental Romanesque style was not however of long duration. It disappeared with the radical change in western architecture, the advent of the Gothic church. The increased window space of the lofty cathedral replaced wall painting with the 'picture' of stained glass. Sculpture took pride of place as a representational art. Painting was largely confined to the book scale, the illumination of the service and prayer-books, missals and Books of House. There was a change, however, in the attitude of the artist (and of his wealthy patrons), a delight in fine detail, gay colour, in human character and the appearance of nature, which had previously been lacking. Its qualities appear in the altarpieces and other works which applied the style of manuscript painting to a larger scale. Altarpieces were executed in tempara, a medium related to the opaque water-colour of the illuminated manuscript, but a new and glorious future for painting came with the development of the oil medium in the 15th century. The paintings of Jan van Eyck (c. 1390–1441), who worked at Bruges, represent the climax of the detailed and beautiful Gothic style and an early perfection of oil painting.

The Renaissance

In Italy the Gothic style never took a strong hold. Church building was not drastically changed in character as it was in France and England. Artists continued to produce wall-paintings on a large scale and masterpieces were produced in constant succession from the end of the 13th century onwards. At the same time there was a change of outlook which attained its full development in the 16th century and is indicated by the word 'Renaissance'. Strictly speaking it means 'rebirth', and in art it refers to a revived interest in the classic productions of the ancient world. Thus the human figure which the artists of the Middle Ages had shunned once again became the artist's main subject.

This, however, was only one aspect of the Renaissance. It marked the end of the Middle Ages in another way: in the growth of a desire for knowledge and the spirit of science. Artists began to study anatomy and the effects of light and shadow, which made their work more life-like. These studies were practised all the more freely because of a growing taste among the Italian patrons of art for other than religious subjects, for example those taken from classical myth in which the artist could group at his discretion nude and clothed figures, buildings and landscape. Botticelli is one of the great examples.

The heyday of the Renaissance is to be placed between the 15th and 16th centuries in Italy, and its great representatives are Leonardo da Vinci, Michelangelo, Raphael, Giorgione, Titian and Tintoretto. They used the perfected science of painting to create harmonies and rhythms of unsurpassed majesty and beauty.

Baroque and Rococo

Two international styles followed the Renaissance. The first is known as Baroque. It is marked by dramatic gesture and movement and was often a sort of imposing propaganda for Church and State. The work of the great Flemish painter Rubens in the 17th century provides an outstanding example of this style. It was followed in the 18th century by Rococo, a graceful and artificial mode of interior decoration, and lighter in style, exemplified for example in the paintings of the French artists, Boucher and Fragonard.

The National Schools

The observer will note that the foregoing international terms do not refer to painting alone but also to architecture and sculpture and minor forms of art and craftsmanship, such as tapestries and furniture. For a great church or the palace of a king or prince a consistent style was required. It was to some extent independent, at this princely and ecclesiastical level, from differences of race and nationality. Meanwhile, however, these differences, together with growing variations in religious beliefs and types of society, tended to produce national 'schools' of art. A 'school' implies a number of painters working in the same region whose work has some general likeness of style and outlook. Each of the main countries of Europe has, at one period or another, produced such groups of artists, whose work is not only of outstanding interest but distinct in its regional and national character.

Thus *Italy* is not only the country of the great movement called the Renaissance; it represents also a whole series of schools which grew up in the various city states into which the country was anciently divided—Florence, Siena, Parma, Venice and so on. *Florence* was astonishingly rich in great artists. They include Giotto, Fran Angelico, Botticelli, Leonardo and Michelangelo to mention only a few whose fame is universal. In Florence the 'scientific attitude which enabled the artist to represent convincingly the weight and dignity of form in the round was cultivated to the highest degree. In this sense the Florentine genius may be called sculptural. *Venice* was the centre of another great school—here again there is a long list of famous artists, including Giovanni Bellini, Carpaccio, Giorgione, Titian, Tintoretto, Veronese and in the 18th century, Canaletto and Guardi. The Venetian School is noted for its rich colour and a more sensuous character than that of the intellectual Florentines. In the 16th century *Bologna* was the centre of a school that tried to pick out and combine the best qualities of a number of the earliest masters. *Naples* in the 17th century was the centre of a rather sombre *Spanish-Italian School* of whom Ribera is typical.

The great period of the Southern Netherlands, the *Flemish School* extends from the 15th to the 17th century, though it has two distinct aspects. There is first the highly detailed and mainly religious art (though including portraiture) of the early masters, van Eyck, van der Weyden and Memlinc and secondly the florid and vigorous art, varied in subject matter, which is supremely represented by Rubens.

The *Dutch School* is the product of one century, the 17th, in which the northern provinces of the Netherlands attained their independence. It is marked by a strongly national feeling and pride in its middle-class prosperity, its well kept interiors, its characteristic flat landscape, its flowers. The Dutch greatly developed portraiture, landscape and still-life and gave to art two of its greatest masters in Rembrandt and Vermeer.

French painting reaches a sustained level from the 17th to the 19th century. Centrally placed between north and south Europe, France was influenced both by Italian and Flemish art, though developing a strong individuality, to be seen in such great masters as Nicolas Poussin and Claude, Watteau, Chardin and Fragonard. A brilliant succession of painters in the 19th century, from Corot and Delacroix to Manet and the Impressionists, makes this perhaps the most remarkable period of all in French painting.

The great period of *British Painting* is from the early 18th to the early 19th century. Beginning with Hogarth and his pictures of social life, it comprises the achievements in portraiture of Gainsborough, Reynolds and others, and in landscape of Wilson, Gainsborough, Crome, Turner and Constable; while its school of water-colour painting was a growth without parallel elsewhere.

German art flowered in the 16th century, combining the Gothic passion for detail with an intense earnestness that did not shrink from ugliness. The great artists of this period are Matthias Grunewald, who added a masterpiece to European painting in his *Isenheim Altarpiece*, and Albrecht Durer whose engravings and drawings are among the great classics of art.

The genius of *Spain* likewise is concentrated in a few men of outstanding greatness: El Greco in the late 16th century, Velazquez, who in achievement and influence is one of the greatest of all, and finally Goya with his keen social vision.

1. In the Gothic period sculpture took pride of place as a representational art.   True   False
2. Gothic art produced a new attitude in the artist.   True   False
3. In Italy the Gothic style never took a strong hold.   True   False
4. In Italy artists produced wall paintings on a large scale and masterpieces were produced in constant succession from the end of the 13th century onwards.   True   False
5. The change of outlook known as the Renaissance attained its full development in the 13th century.   True   False
6. Renaissance means re-birth.   True   False
7. In the Renaissance the human figure became the artist's main subject.   True   False
8. The study of anatomy, light and shadow, although important, did not make Renaissance art more life-like.   True   False
9. Baroque and Rococo were national styles that followed the Renaissance.   True   False
10. Baroque and Rococo were, respectively, dramatic and graceful.   True   False
11. Italy had only one, rather than a series of schools of art.   True   False
12. The Dutch school greatly developed portraiture and landscapes.   True   False
13. French painting was greatly influenced by Italian and Flemish art.   True   False
14. The great period of English painting lasted 300 years.   True   False
15. German art flowered in the 16th century.   True   False

CHAPTER SIXTEEN

ADVANCED TECHNIQUES

Up to this point I have dealt with traditional reading problems and approaches, shedding where possible new light on these areas. I have mentioned, at various stages, the Advanced Reading Techniques that are being taught by institutes in America, and by The College of Advanced Reading in England.

These techniques cannot be learned properly from a book. Continued and regular supervision is required from qualified instructors.

What I *can* do is to introduce the subject, explaining something of the fundamental principles, and start you on the first steps to these Advanced Methods. Even using these *basic* hints, many of you will notice considerable improvement in your already improved speed.

The underlying concept of the Advanced Techniques is that the visual field (the area of space we normally see) can be used more effectively in the reading process. You will remember that in Chapter 2 I explained that your focus could be stretched *along* the line in order to take in more words at a glance. Advanced Reading proponents, and I am one of them, see no reason why a reader cannot make use of his *vertical* vision as well while reading. After all, when we look at peoples' faces we do not look 'along a line'; we see an area which we fully absorb. Why not do the same with print?

I have diagrammed the field of vision, showing the various steps in the development of this more inclusive focusing ability:

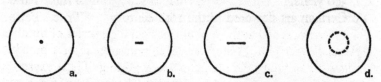

Fig. 6. a. Focus on a single letter, as when a child first learns to read by the phonic method. b. Focus on a single word (the poor-to-average reader). c. Focus on 4–5 words at a time (the good reader). d. Focus on groups or bunches of words (the Advanced Reader)

As I have mentioned, it is not possible for us here to develop a complete Advanced Reading Technique; but it is possible to *begin*.

The first step, and this may surprise you, is to use your hand as a guide! Circle the thumb and fore-finger of your right hand, extend the other three fingers into a straight wedge, and with the palm upwards place your hand at an angle of $45°$ on the page. Commencing at the first line, smoothly sweep the tip of the wedge along that line, lift your hand about a $\frac{1}{4}''$ off the page and go back to the beginning of the next line where once again your finger-nails should just touch the page. Repeat this movement along the next line, get to the end, lift off the page, return, and so on.

It is important in this first stage to make sure that the movement is continuous and smooth, with no pauses or jerks at the end or beginning of lines.

Once you have mastered this movement, keeping your wrist, elbow and shoulder very relaxed, gradually speed up until your hand is going as fast as possible, and you have lost *all* comprehension. Repeat this exercise a number of times, and then go back for a normal reading moving the hand underneath the lines at a comfortable pace. Within a few days many of you will have doubled your already improved speeds.

When you have achieved facility with this step, you will be ready to try the next leap forward, which is to make use of a wider area of focus, as mentioned earlier. The exercise is similar to the one you have just completed, but instead of sweeping your hand under only one line, you sweep it under *two at a time*. This may prove extremely difficult at first, as you are using entirely new visual techniques, but as usual perseverance will bring its reward.

I have diagrammed overleaf the hand position to be used, and the movement the hand should make.

I have included at the end of this chapter a series of number exercises which will help you develop awareness of a possible wider use of your field of vision when reading. These exercises are similar to the number exercises in Chapter 6 but force you to use the vertical part of your vision as well as the linear.

The chapter you have just finished reading has introduced you to techniques which hold the possibility of doubling your

already improved reading performance! Before taking the next
Self Test, practise the Advanced Techniques thoroughly, and

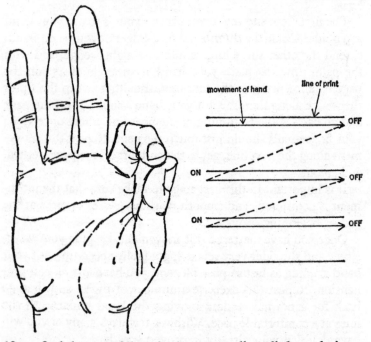

if you find them useful apply them, as well as all the techniques
you have previously learnt, to the following article on Astronomy.

SELF TEST 9
ASTRONOMY

Ancient Readings of the Sky

The study of astronomy began when man, in his curiosity,
made a significant discovery about celestial movements: they
measured time. The sun fixed day and night and the sequence
of the seasons. The moon and stars told the passage of the
night-time hours. Calendars based on these regular cycles were
devised in Babylon and Egypt long before 2500 B.C. The
Egyptians divided their crop year into three seasons and always
marked its beginning when the star Sirius appeared at a certain
spot in the eastern sky. When Sirius showed up, it meant the
Nile was about to flood. Much later the Maya of Central

America used solar observations to set the time for burning off their cornfields before each year's planting, and checked their calendar against measurements of the motions of Venus.

The Emerging Celestial Patterns

It did not take early sky watchers long to realize that the arrangement of the heavens was not chaotic but had a systematic pattern. The stars hung in the sky in fixed groups, and certain groups in succession always came up in the east just before sunrise. Astronomers deduced that these constellations stretched in a belt around the circle of the heavens, and that the sun, in its apparent annual trip about the earth, always stayed within that belt. The belt constellations eventually were given names and became the 12 figures, or signs, of the zodiac. The zodiac was used, and still is, by astrologers, to foretell events in the lives of men and nations.

A different sort of celestial pattern was worked out by Greek astronomers in an attempt to explain the heavenly movements. This concept, perfected by Ptolemy, saw the sun, moon and planets moving around the earth in complex orbits. Ingenious and well-supported by the evidence of men's eyes, the Ptolemaic theory prevailed for another 13 centuries.

The Copernican Revolt

In the 16th Century the work of two men helped to destroy the Ptolemaic idea of an earth-centred universe which had been accepted everywhere for 1,300 years. In 1543 Nicholas Copernicus, a brilliant Polish lawyer and astronomer, turned the old idea around by insisting that 'in the centre of everything the sun must reside . . . where he can give light to all the planets'. Although Copernicus mistakenly assumed that the planets followed perfect circle orbits, all the facts then known about the solar system were much more simply explained by his sun-centred theory than by Ptolemy's. The old ideas died hard, however, and not until the next century was the revolutionary concept accepted.

What ultimately was to be vital to the proof of the Copernican system was the work of a Danish astronomer, Tycho Brahe. Unlike Copernicus, Tycho was a measurer rather than a theoretician, and he designed astronomical instruments larger and more carefully engineered than any that had ever been used before. He built a remarkable observatory in 1576 and spent 21 years there making observations and calculations of the stars and planets with astonishing precision. Tycho himself clung to an earth-centred theory, but his research, in the hands of later scientists, helped to prove the new Copernican notions of the universe.

Enter the Telescope

When Galileo turned his primitive telescope to the sky in 1609, he saw things which men had hardly dreamed were there. He found mountains on the moon; he saw that Venus had moon-like phases which proved its sun-centred orbit. With that, the old, comforting idea of a centrally located earth was doomed. Meanwhile, in Prague, mathematician Johannes Kepler, using Tycho Brahe's measurements, calculated the planets' elliptical orbits about the sun, and upset the old concept of the circle as the typical celestial form. By observation and deduction, Kepler framed the basic laws of the solar system as it is known now, and shaped astronomy's future.

Stargazers of the East

Though science was all but blotted out in Europe during the Dark Ages, the world's accumulation of knowledge about astronomy was not lost. Both in India (from about A.D. 250) and in the Moslem world (starting four centuries later), astronomers kept on observing and calculating—and finding nothing to contradict Ptolemy's theories. Through the centuries they kept on refining all the basic instruments of naked-eye observation, such as the astrolable for measuring stars' positions and the gnomon, or sundial, which shows the sun's movement by shadows.

Knowledge gained at observatories in Alexandria and Baghdad was carried westward to Europe and eastward to China. In India, meanwhile, astronomical efforts reached a monumental peak with the work of the 18th Century astronomer Jai Singh II, who realized that the larger his observational instruments were, the more accurate they would be. He built the structures which are the biggest and perhaps the best ever made for naked-eye observations.

One thing that limited medieval astronomers was the very elastic concept of time that most societies had. The day was divided conveniently enough into 12 hours, measured from the time the sun came up to when it set. The trouble was an hour in a midsummer day was a good deal longer than an hour in midwinter. Further, the only timekeepers were sundials—useless on cloudy days—and even less precise devices that operated by water power. This state of affairs was increasingly bothersome to astronomers who, by the 16th Century had begun to need accurate timing for their observations.

Fortunately the metal-working and mechanical skills of Renaissance craftsmen were beginning to produce clocks for noblemen and scientists. In 1362, Giovanni de Dondi finished an astronomical clock that not only told time but also recorded the movements of the planets with an extraordinarily complicated gear train. De Doni's masterpiece, the oldest known European mechanical clock, was the forerunner of a clockwork revolution which, in a few centuries, was producing beautiful intruments.

TEST 9 (980 words)

1. The study of astronomy began when Man discovered that celestial movements measured time.   True - False

2. Egyptian and Mayan civilisations used astronomy to regulate their agriculture.   True   False

3. Early sky watchers realised that the arrangement of the heavens was chaotic.   True   False

4. The zodiac refers to the star Sirius.   True   False

5. Ptolemy perfected the Greek concept of astronomy which saw the sun, moon and planets moving around the earth.   True - False

6. Ptolemy's theory prevailed for 1,300 years.   True - False

7. During the Dark Ages the study of astronomy was universally abandoned.   True   False

8. One thing that limited medieval astronomers was the elastic concept of time that most societies had.   True   False

9. In medieval times the only time-keepers were sun-dials.   True   False

10. The first astronomical clock was made by the Romans.   True   False

11. Nicholas Corpenicus taught that the planets orbitted the sun.   True   False

12. The work of Tycho Brahe was concerned with astronomical measurement.   True   False

13. Tycho Brahe agreed with the Copernican theory.   True   False

14. Galileo turned his telescope to the sky in 1909.   True   False

15. Johannes Kepler framed the basic laws of the solar system.   True   False

27		84	
91	....	20	....
93		13	
06	....	67	....
92		34	
11	....	55	....
85		47	
73	....	98	....
05		17	
92	....	09	....
56		38	
71	....	50	....
29		73	
65	....	32	....
72		83	
15	....	27	....

02		99	
47	....	31	....
70		38	
94	....	17	....
38		46	
67	....	12	....
95		69	
03	....	14	....
52		93	
17	....	74	....
07		28	
41	....	64	....
60		14	
29	....	96	....
13		57	
09	....	26	....
84		32	
26	....	81	....
97		04	
35	....	58	....
82		74	
41	....	90	....
19		66	
95	....	12	....
10		64	
86	....	27	....

73
19 ....

47
04 ....

76
23 ....

19
75 ....

43
12 ....

06
84 ....

36
74 ....

40
39 ....

38
14 ....

82
39 ....

55
13 ....

93
015 ....

17
963 ....

49
21 ....

92
61 ....

11
97 ....

62
59 ....

51
98 ....

19
58 ....

45
51 ....

77
69 ....

72
30 ....

13
76 ....

92
35 ....

17
935 ....

92
147 ....

67 921	....	24 095	....
45 920	....	83 694	....
03 961	....	97 276	....
48 762	....	76 193	....
90 216	....	03 184	....
85 102	....	26 975	....
92 183	....	59 413	....
37 628	....	21 049	....
75 941	....	82 457	....
84 307	....	49 562	....
18 592	....	94 165	....
89 062	....	14 830	....
56 107	....	93 724	....

02
733 ....

75
916 ....

07
825 ....

81
943 ....

28
921 ....

42
105 ....

63
429 ....

90
472 ....

65
917 ....

93
059 ....

45
298 ....

36
275 ....

06
329 ....

64
190 ....

93
076 ....

23
196 ....

36
741 ....

94
566 ....

56
029 ....

93
575 ....

38
470 ....

21
349 ....

31
280 ....

17
503 ....

94
705 ....

19
062 ....

12 965	....	29 410	....
94 562	....	83 391	....
51 379	....	77 152	....
49 063	....	71 926	....
10 692	....	62 831	....
694 801	....	591 032	....
937 804	....	152 407	....
462 591	....	915 862	....
905 817	....	105 762	....
952 831	....	908 752	....
328 947	....	462 731	....
920 153	....	072 394	....
845 701	....	862 143	....

565		721	
928	....	038	....
724		157	
016	....	924	....
416		625	
539	....	948	....
286		483	
910	....	109	....
083		956	
926	....	431	....
167		762	
528	....	457	....
062		197	
873	....	035	....
941		482	
570	....	191	....
731		397	
162	....	143	....
492		920	
184	....	413	....
525		937	
182	....	013	....
710		062	
392	....	493	....
511		507	
936	....	341	....

829		173	
147	....	672	....
601		724	
934	....	162	....
290		407	
174	....	852	....
783		590	
420	....	743	....
593		421	
207	....	905	....
439		806	
617	....	944	....
127		704	
482	....	911	....
057		613	
982	....	936	....
162		730	
974	....	146	....
804		852	
193	....	901	....
253		394	
109	....	706	....

CHAPTER SEVENTEEN

SUMMARY AND ADVICE FOR THE FUTURE

Your reading course is nearing its end!

Over the past weeks (and I hope, in not too many cases, few months) you have covered a considerable amount of information some of which you may still be consolidating.

In the early chapters you were introduced to the basic physiology of eye movement, and to the very real reading problems which face most people. In addition, the major areas of concentration, comprehension, and reading conditions were introduced.

You were introduced also to the first of the self-tests. As mentioned in the Preface, these tests dealt with the basic areas of human knowledge, and they were by no means easy. They represent the meatiest kind of material you are likely to be faced with in your general reading and also perhaps in your study reading. If you have managed to improve your word-per-minute score on these tests, you have done well. (Many books on speed reading have 'improvement tests' that use either very easy material or material only a few paragraphs long. In either case the 'excellent' scores from such tests are not valid, for they do not test you thoroughly or in a reading situation similar to normal reading.)

I hope that the self-tests have not only enabled you to gauge your progress, but have also encouraged you to read more widely. *All* subjects are interesting as long as you know how to approach them.

By the time you were well into the book, the first of the vocabulary chapters had been introduced and you were on the way to becoming a reader who was aware not only of the general background and basic theory in the field, but who was also consciously improving the basic material with which one deals: the words themselves. Although this is the final chapter this does not mean that your vocabulary training and improvement should cease. I hope that you have already made the study of words and the expansion of your vocabulary a part of every-day life.

As the book progressed you were introduced to techniques such as skimming and scanning that enabled you to get an over-view of your reading material. This was eventually combined with the concept of previewing and further supported by a discussion of the way in which paragraphs are structured and material is presented. Critical analysis and logic are added to your artillery.

In Chapter 13, The Buzan Study Technique, most of the concepts and ideas of which you had learnt up to this point were integrated into a study system that is new and comprehensive. Using this system you can study any subject, ranging from the finest literature to the most profound and complex philosophy and science.

As the book neared this final chapter, you were introduced for the first time to the Advanced Techniques taught by such institutes as The College of Advanced Reading, which are now sweeping the field of Advanced Reading. It is obvious that these techniques need to be taught under direct instructor supervision, but the material you have been given in this book lays the perfect groundwork for such a course.

At the end of this chapter is one more self-test on *Communication*. While reading it, bring to bear *all* the relevant knowledge you have gained from this book, and try to surpass your previous performances.

One final word: come back to this final word again soon! In other words, when you have finished the book *Postview* it—it will enable you to integrate all you have learned and to realise that you possess the background and knowledge to become an active and experienced reader who can approach any reading task with buoyancy and confidence.

SELF TEST 10

COMMUNICATIONS

Considering the importance of language in the development of human society, it is astonishing to find how little is known about its origins. Writing, which by definition is a lasting record, occurred quite late in human history, but speech, which is by nature evanescent, may have arisen tens of thousands of years before writing first appeared. Who knows what language, if any, was spoken by paleolithic man he whose bones, whose tools, whose paintings on the walls of caves have survived, but not his speech? The absence of any real evidence for the origin of human speech has opened the subject up to endless speculation. There were always those, of course, who held that speech was divinely revealed to man, a gift from God. Others more logical but no less wide of the mark—including Democritus, Locke, Condillac, and Adam Smith—held that speech was adopted by Mankind in convention; in other words that it might be looked upon as an artificial creation legislated, so to speak, into existence.

From the nineteenth century onward, research into the original of speech increased in quantity, seriousness, and intensity—but the results were as meager as ever. Among recent scholars several alternative theories have arisen and have been given colourful names which should not detract from their serious intent. There is, for instance, the 'bow-wow' theory, which holds that human words first arose from imitations of natural sounds such as the barking of a dog. Or the 'pooh-pooh' theory, that speech began with exclamations of fear, pain, pleasure, and the like, and its close relative the 'yo-he-ho' theory, that it started with grunts of physical exertion, or the 'sing-song' theory, holding that primitive chants opened the way to speech. The Soviet scholar Marr considers that articulate speech began as an accompaniment to communication by gesture. And he bases all variations and combinations in subsequent speech on only four primitive sounds originally used with these gestures—sol, ber, yon, and rok. Other linguists believe that speech appears only when as with children, a person's mental activity attains a certain level of development.

All of this admirable scholarship does little to clarify the actual origin of language. In fact, most of it is just as speculative as the persistent legend that the first and original language was the 'language of the birds'. This bizarre idea crops up among the ancient Egyptians, among the Incas of South America, and in the stories of Orpheus, Siegfried and St. Francis of Assisi. It was quite seriously discussed by the medieval alchemist Fulcanelli, who wrote, 'Those rare writers who have spoken of the "language of the birds" accord it first place in the origins of speech. They say that it goes back to Adam, who used it to impose under God's will suitable names designed to define the characteristics of the people and things of creation.'

The idea that there must have been *some* original language is as persistent as the legend of the 'language of the birds'. Up to the end of the seventeenth century, Hebrew, the language of divine revelation, was held to be the original language of humanity. Leibnitz protested vigorously against this view, and gradually emphasis shifted from a search for the single original language to the fact, which was becoming increasingly obvious, that there were groups, or families, of languages. In attempting to unravel the relationships that linked the various tongues scholars began to develop a new tool for the study of the origin and diffusion of languages. Historical and comparative linguistics, especially as applied to the problem of the Indo-European group of languages in the nineteenth century, began to provide a far sounder and more scientific basis for the study of language in general.

Years of careful and devoted scholarship have built up a picture of the world's languages, living and dead, which is almost frightening in its complexity. It is estimated that at the present time there are some 3,000 languages currently in use. In Europe alone scholars count 120. Then there are the dead languages, including Sumerian, Sanskrit, Avestan, Latin, Phoenician, Scythian, Iberian, and the rest. Altogether, it seems that almost 4,000 languages have disappeared during the course of human, and thus lingual, evolution. A strange example is the Etruscan, which can be read because it was written in a Greek script, but understood very little or not at all because its syntax differs from that of every known language.

And all these languages, living and dead—except for a few, such as the Baswue and the Japanese Ainu, which so far have defied classification—are complexly interrelated, through common origins, similar structure, word roots, and word sounds, thus falling into family groups, and subdivisions of these groups, some enormous, some quite insignificant. The largest overall groupings are the African, Semitic-Hamitic, Indo-European, Sino-Tibetan, Japanese-Korean, Ural-Altaic Austronesian, North American Indian, and South American Indian. To these, many other groups and subgroups may be added ad infinitum: the Caucasian, the Dravidian, the Finno-Ugrian, 26 smaller families from North America, including Eskimo, Algonquin, Uto-Aztec and Iroquois, 20 from Central America including Mayan and Zapotecan, and 77 from South America and the West Indies, including Arawak, Carib, and Chibcha. The count for the classification of the numerous Indian languages is still in an embryonic state.

Of these so-called 'families' of languages, some may be spoken by mere thousands of people, whereas the Sino-Tibetan languages of southeastern Asia are spoken by well over 600 million people, and the Indo-Iranian languages by some 400 million. Yet the latter is merely one subgroup of the great Indo-European, or Aryan, family of languages, which includes numerous other subgroups, such as the Germanic, Romance, Slavic, and lesser units like the Greek, Albanian, and Armenian.

The Indo-European family of languages, now used by about half of the world's population, is supposed to have stemmed from a small, compact area—variously located from the Iranian plateau through Central Europe to the Baltic—whose inhabitants migrated south and westwards before 2000 B.C., spreading the basic structure of their language to many diverse areas. Much later, Latin, a minor Indo-European dialect centered near the mouth of the Tiber River, spread by conquest over most of Europe and the Mediterranean. Offshoots of Latin and of the Germanic subgroup of the Indo-European family—French, Spanish, and English—have now travelled around the world. Yet the close relationships of the many widespread branches of the Indo-European is nevertheless still quite clear. Travellers to Iran, for instance, are astonished to find that such basic words as 'mother' and 'father' are almost the same as in English.

Such a picture of languages and language groups growing and dying, evolving, splitting, competing, ever active and ever changing, seems utterly confusing until it is remembered that language is merely an expression of human society. Languages, like cultures, nations, and civilizations, tend to disintegrate into local groupings unless there is a strong centralizing influence to enforce unity and growth. The Romans spread Latin around the known world, but when the Roman Empire broke up, Latin, too, diverged into the various Romance languages we know today. Languages follow social, political, economic, and religious trends. Dying languages for instance, have been revived for political reasons—as in Ireland and Israel. Even within a given language area, differences in dialect, usage, and vocabulary will reflect the fine shadings of class differences, of the differences between young and old, and between one profession and another. Language is indeed a form of social behaviour.

1. Astonishingly little is known about the origins of language.   True   False
2. Writing occurred early in human history.   True   False
3. Democritus, Locke, Condillac and Adam Smith saw 'speech' as an artificial creation.   True   False
4. The pooh-pooh theory holds that human words first arose from imitations of natural sounds such as the barking of a dog.   True   False
5. Much of the scholarship and theoretical suggestion on language does little to clarify its origin.   True   False
6. Research into language is called 'hieroglyphics'.   True   False
7. Until the 17th century the original language of mankind was thought to be Hebrew.   True   False
8. Leibnitz supported the theory that Hebrew was the original language of mankind.   True   False
9. Historical and comparative linguistics provided a sounder and more scientific basis for the study of language.   True   False
10. In Europe 120 languages are current.   True   False
11. The Baswue and the Japanese Ainu language were among those that were easy to classify.   True   False
12. The Indo-European group of languages are spoken by half the world's population.   True   False
13. Latin was a minor Indo-European dialect centred near the mouth of the Tiber river.   True   False
14. The relationship of the widespread branches of the Indo-European language is now not very clear.   True   False
15. Languages follow social, political, economic and religious trends.   True   False

Self Test 1
1.T 2.F 3.F 4.F 5.T 6.T 7.F 8.F 9.F 10.T
11.F 12.F 13.T 14.F 15.T

Self Test 2
1.F 2.T 3.F 4.F 5.F 6.F 7.T 8.F 9.F 10.T
11.F 12.F 13.F 14.F 15.F

Self Test 3
1.F 2.T 3.F 4.T 5.T 6.F 7.F 8.F 9.F 10.F
11.T 12.F 13.T 14.T 15.T

Self Test 4
1.T 2.T 3.F 4.F 5.T 6.T 7.T 8.F 9.F 10.T
11.F 12.F 13.T 14.F 15.F

Self Test 5
1.T 2.F 3.T 4.F 5.F 6.T 7.F 8.F 9.F 10.T
11.F 12.F 13.T 14.F 15.F

Self Test 6
1.F 2.T 3.T 4.T 5.F 6.F 7.T 8.T 9.F 10.T
11.T 12.T 13.F 14.T 15.F

Self Test 7
1.T 2.T 3.F 4.T 5.T 6.F 7.T 8.F 9.F 10.F
11.T 12.T 13.F 14.F 15.T

Self Test 8
1.T 2.T 3.T 4.T 5.F 6.T 7.T 8.F 9.F 10.T
11.F 12.T 13.T 14.F 15.T

Self Test 9
1.T 2.T 3.F 4.F 5.T 6.T 7.F 8.T 9.T 10.F
11.T 12.T 13.F 14.T 15.T

Self Test 10
1.T 2.F 3.T 4.F 5.T 6.F 7.T 8.F 9.T 10.T
11.F 12.T 13.T 14.F 15.T

VOCABULARY EXERCISE ANSWERS

Chapter 4
Exercise 1
1.l 2.e 3.m 4.f 5.n 6.g 7.o 8.d 9.k 10.c 11.j
12.b 13.i 14.a 15.h

Exercise 2
1.e 2.i 3.d 4.n 5.j 6.f 7.k 8.c 9.a 10.l 11.g
12.o 13.m 14.h 15.b
Exercise 3
1.h 2.a 3.o 4.b 5.k 6.c 7.n 8.d 9.l 10.m 11.g
12.j 13.f 14.i 15.e
Chapter 11
Exercise 1
1.f 2.l 3.k 4.i 5.e 6.h 7.d 8.n 9.m 10.a 11.j
12.b 13.g 14.c 15.o
Exercise 2
1.o 2.h 3.a 4.b 5.m 6.n 7.f 8.d 9.j 10.f 11.g
12.k 13.i 14.l 15.c
Exercise 3
1.o 2.f 3.c 4.n 5.m 6.i 7.k 8.a 9.j 10.l 11.b
12.e 13.g 14.d 15.h
Chapter 15
Exercise 1
1.h 2.d 3.b 4.l 5.e 6.n 7.a 8.j 9.m 10.o 11.g
12.i 13.c 14.k 15.f
Exercise 2
1.d 2.a 3.k 4.h 5.j 6.l 7.n 8.m 9.o 10.b 11.g
12.f 13.c 14.e 15.i
Exercise 3
1.e 2.k 3.d 4.l 5.a 6.o 7.i 8.n 9.m 10.j 11.g
12.b 13.c 14.f 15.h

SPEED READING GRAPH

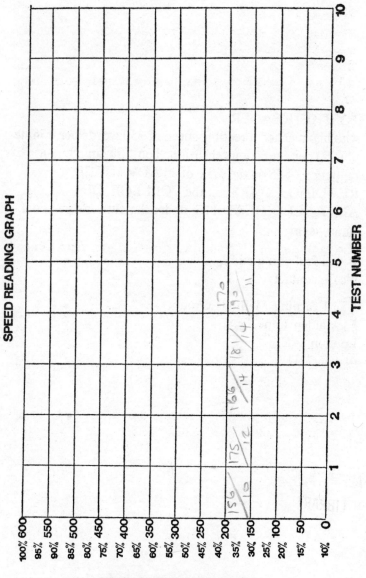

SPEED & COMPREHENSION

TEST NUMBER

TO THE READER
who has reached a reading speed of 350 words per minute
plus 50 per cent comprehension, Tony Buzan offers a
reduction of £5 on the price of an ADVANCED
READING COURSE at the COLLEGE OF
ADVANCED READING, under the author's personal
supervision.

If you feel you qualify,
please contact:

The Learning Methods Group,
33 Maiden Lane,
London WC2
01-836-7211